Anger Management:
TRANSFORM
Anger into Advantage

R. Lance Parker, Ph.D.

ISBN 979-8-89428-562-7 (paperback)
ISBN 979-8-89428-993-9 (hardcover)
ISBN 979-8-89428-563-4 (digital)

Copyright © 2024 by R. Lance Parker, Ph.D.

All rights reserved. No part of this publication may be reproduced, distributed, or transmitted in any form or by any means, including photocopying, recording, or other electronic or mechanical methods without the prior written permission of the publisher. For permission requests, solicit the publisher via the address below.

Christian Faith Publishing
832 Park Avenue
Meadville, PA 16335
www.christianfaithpublishing.com

Printed in the United States of America

Dedication

Over the years, many who attended my anger management seminars and classes urged me to write a book outlining and explaining this unique approach to anger management and share it with others. This constant encouragement, coupled with witnessing so many people successfully transform their lives, gave me the courage to finally write this book.

For my wife, Tish, who has shown great patience with my quirkiness and still encourages me to pursue my dreams, thank you for giving me the push and the freedom to write.

And for my son who, after all these years, is still teaching me what is truly important in this life, *Ryan, you are the best son ever!*

A truly effective approach to harnessing your power
for a better life. Real solutions, real results.

—R. Lance Parker, PhD,
Licensed Psychologist

Contents

Introduction: The Purpose of This Book ix

Chapter 1: What Is Anger? 1
Chapter 2: The Anger Model 10
Chapter 3: Boundaries 21
Chapter 4: Perceptions—Should 33
Chapter 5: Perceptions—Jumping to Conclusions 50
Chapter 6: Emotional Well-Being 58
Chapter 7: Assertiveness 73
Chapter 8: Listening 84
Chapter 9: Bringing It All Together 92

Anger-Management Model Template 103

Introduction

The Purpose of This Book

If you're reading this book, you probably have been told you have a problem with anger. And if you're like most people who have been told they have a problem with anger, you probably don't think you have a problem with anger. Or maybe you picked up this book because someone you know has a problem with anger, and you're looking for a way to help them or understand them. In any case, the most important thing to keep in mind as you read this book is *anger is good*. So make it your *advantage*.

All your life, you have been taught that anger was bad. You have been told, "You're too angry," or "You need to get it under control," or "You shouldn't feel so angry." Somehow, if you're angry, you are bad. Maybe you have begun to accept this notion as true and believe it yourself. You feel yourself becoming angry, then you become frustrated with yourself for being angry. Maybe you feel like giving up because you're unable to stop getting angry. Maybe you're beginning to think that everyone else is right and that you are truly a bad person.

Many who read this book have tried (or been made to try) various medications. Some doctors view anger as a symptom of a mental illness, and you may have been diagnosed with Major Depressive Disorder or Bipolar Affective Disorder. Maybe the medication worked. Often, it doesn't. And when the medication doesn't work, you get locked into a cycle of trying a different medication, waiting to see if it helps, and if it doesn't, then you have to wean off of that medication and give another one a try and wait again. How do you know if it is working? Don't worry. Others will tell you. So you have to see what the doctor says, try a new medication, suffer the side effects, listen to family talk about how you are doing, and try a different medication if they don't believe this medication is helping. Bottom line, you have no control over your life, and your opinion is the least important thing considered.

Still, others of you may have taken an Anger Management class. (That was fun, wasn't it?) There you were, sitting in a room full of "wife beaters" and other "derelicts you wouldn't be caught dead with in any other circumstance" (at least this is what many of my students said they expected their classmates to be like). And why were you in that class anyway? You "don't have a problem." At least, that is what you believed then and maybe still do.

Let me repeat myself: *anger is good*. God gave you this emotion, and he made you in his likeness (Genesis 5:1). To illustrate this point, consider Body Integrity Identity Disorder. This is a rare condition in which a person believes they would be better off having a limb removed. That's right! They want their leg cut off or their arm. Some people want both legs removed, and they know exactly where they want them to end, often drawing lines at the precise point.

Now most of you reading this are thinking, *That is crazy!* The reason you think this crazy is because you recognize God made you with two legs and two arms, and the system seems to work very well. When you use your legs as designed, they help you live a good life. You stand, walk, and run. You might even exercise your legs to improve how well you get about. You have probably never considered intentionally getting rid of a foot or a shin or a leg.

But while you call these people crazy, you sit there hoping this book will help get rid of your anger. Does this make any more sense? God never makes mistakes (2 Samuel 22:33), and everything God has created is good (Genesis 1:31), so that means *anger is good*.

Think about how difficult life would be if you did not have two legs. Some of you already know how that feels. Maybe you injured your ankle and had to use crutches while you healed. Suddenly, getting from the house to the car is very difficult. As long as you use both legs as designed, that part of life is pretty easy, but if you were to intentionally try to live life as if you did not have the use of one of your legs, life would become very difficult very quickly.

It is the same with anger. The problem only arises when you try to not have anger, when you try to suppress the urge to yell or scream. The problem arises when you vent, letting off steam in unproductive directions. That is the problem. The problem arises when you try to make others do what they are *supposed* to do or try to *make* them understand why they are wrong or try to *make* them feel what it feels like to you. This, too, is the problem. The problem arises when you get angry and sit and whine and moan about how *unfair* life is or how others have done you wrong. These are the problems, not anger.

Anger is good because it was given to you by God, but you have to understand what the purpose of anger is and how to use anger as it was designed. When you do that, anger actually makes your life better. It makes the lives of your family better. It strengthens relationships. It increases your self-esteem and improves how others see you.

What I propose is that you stop wasting your time trying to rid your life of anger or using the anger to control others or to validate your own misery. I suggest you come to understand the purpose of this powerful emotion and then harness that power to exert more effective control over your life, improve your relationship with others, and begin to actually feel better.

Ironically, when you use your anger in an effective manner to solve problems and resolve conflict, it is not called anger. It is called drive, determination, perseverance, resoluteness, resolve, seriousness, solidness, steadfastness, strong-mindedness, being strong-willed, tenacity, being unfaltering, being unflinching, being unhesitating, or being unwavering. It becomes your *advantage*.

This book will lay out for you a step-by-step process for understanding anger. You will see how anger fits into the overall picture and come to understand the purpose of anger and how to use it effectively.

A student in one of my anger-management classes once commented, "It seems like we are not talking about anger very much in here." He was correct. Because the problem is not *anger* but everything else, such as distorted perceptions, poor boundaries, misunderstood emotions, and a lack of interpersonal skills. Most classes or books on anger try to teach you how to *control* your anger, *turn it off*, or *shut it down*. Some models of anger management mirror the twelve-step programs that are so effective for helping people with alcohol or drug problems. These models require you admit *you are powerless* over your anger. Still others require you admit you are *an abuser*. It is not helpful to shame someone into change. Many people with anger problems have enough shame and guilt as it is. Heaping on more doesn't help. In fact, it usually has the opposite effect.

This book will teach you what anger is, where it comes from, how to evaluate if the anger is necessary, then how to choose what to do with the anger so you can improve your situation, your relationship, and your family. After each chapter, there are study questions. It is extremely important that you answer the study questions before moving on to the next chapter.

As you proceed through this book, I frequently refer to cognitive-reframing skills. Cognitive means *thinking*. Reframing or restructuring means *to change*. Thus, cognitive reframing or cognitive restructuring simply means *change how you think*. In the book *Twelve Two: How to Transform Your Mind*, I provide an in-depth explanation of cognitive restructuring and specific step-by-step tools to begin the process of total transformation by changing how you think. The book focuses on four specific cognitive distortions I refer to as the *Four Fundamentals*. I strongly recommend you get the book *Twelve Two: How to Transform Your Mind* and study it as well. It is available at Amazon, Barnes & Noble, BAM!, or wherever you purchased this book.

ANGER MANAGEMENT:

Introduction Study Questions

1. Take a few moments to write down what problems have been created by the way you presently express your anger.

2. Now write down three things you would like to accomplish in life (career, family, church, etc.).

Chapter 1

What Is Anger?

Many of you are struggling with anger but have no actual idea what it is, so let's answer the question, what is anger? That's easy. Anger is an emotion. Next question.

Why is anger so hard to deal with? That's easy too. Because you don't understand emotions or their purpose. You actively pursue the emotions you like (happiness, joy, excitement) and shun the emotions you don't like (sadness, guilt, anger). Therefore, you're uncomfortable with any amount of sadness, guilt, or anger and act to get rid of it quickly or shut down whatever or whoever you think is *causing* the uncomfortable emotion.

Do you blame other people for these emotions and justify your actions rather than accepting how you feel and using that feeling to improve your life? For example, maybe you have said, "You bet I yelled at her! She did it again, and I have told her a thousand times to stop it! What was I supposed to do? Maybe now she will learn!" Or what about this? "He is really pushing my buttons!" These are examples of blaming others for your anger.

Or how about, "I hate feeling sad, so I don't want to talk about it?" Here, you're not allowing yourself to have emotions in your life simply because they feel uncomfortable.

Maybe you recognize this statement: "I know what I did was wrong, but I said I am sorry, so can we just drop it!?" You try to brush off the guilt quickly so you don't have to feel bad about yourself, then you become angry at them for bringing up something painful. Any of this sounding familiar?

First, you must accept a basic premise. You have emotions for a reason. Nothing about you or your abilities is an accident. Remember, God created you in his *likeness*. Think about that for a moment. He didn't say, "I am perfect the way I am, but I wanted you to be defective, so I threw in these emotions to trip you up." No. He said he made you *in his likeness*, and this is true. If you peruse the Bible, you will see times when God was angry, loving, happy, and sad. We have the capacity to experience a wide variety of emotions because God does, and he knew our lives would be *better* for having the capacity to experience and use these emotions.

==Emotions are the yellow highlighter of life. When you picked up this book and thumbed through it, this paragraph caught your attention because it was highlighted. It caught your attention, and you stopped to look at it to see what was so important about these words that they were highlighted.==

This is what emotions do for your life. They highlight moments, events, or circumstances; bring them to your attention; and *urge* you to respond in a very specific fashion. Without emotions, each moment would be the same as the next. Our lives would be like pages and pages of words on paper. Nothing would jump off the page and catch our attention. Each moment would be experienced exactly as the last moment. There would be no happiness, excitement, sadness, or guilt. Sounds boring, right? Wrong! It couldn't be. There wouldn't even be boredom because that is an emotion too. We would be like robots or computers. There would be no clues as to what is good or bad, desirable or detestable. We would have to analyze events in huge logic sequences to make determinations about what to remember, what to forget, what to do next, and how to respond. Without emotions, we would be paralyzed into inaction. (Paralysis through analysis?)

Let's look at three basic emotions to help you understand how emotions are functional before we discuss anger.

ANGER MANAGEMENT:

Happiness

Oh, we like this feeling. We work hard to create as much happiness in our life as possible—sometimes too hard. The problem is we often don't know what happiness *is*. I ask my patients, "What do you want?" The usual answer I get is, "To be happy," but they can never tell me what happiness actually *is*. When I ask them, it is usually some variation of having some current trial or difficulty come to an end.

Sometimes I will then ask them directly, "What would make you happy?" They struggle here too. They start to tell me a few things that they think might make them happy, but they usually detour into a laundry list of things that would *not* make them happy or what they *don't* want to endure or suffer or tolerate or experience. Sometimes we actually confuse happiness with relief, and the funny thing is relief is not an actual emotion. It is the *absence* of an emotion. For example, I asked one young man who had proclaimed that all he wanted in life was *to be happy*, "What do you think would make you happy?"

He replied, "If I could just get my bills caught up, I would be happy."

But the truth is he would not actually experience happiness. What was really going on is that he was under so much financial pressure that he felt a great deal of stress and anxiety. He believed if he could get rid of the debt, then he would feel happy. This is a fallacy. What he was pursuing is not happiness but relief—*relief* from the pressure of the stress instead of the *addition* of happiness to his life.

If I squeeze your arm, you feel pressure. When I let go, you feel relief. You might even thank me for letting go. But consider what just happened—right now, your arm feels nothing. As I squeeze it, you begin to feel pressure. When I let go, the pressure is *relieved*, and your arm returns to a state of *nothingness*. I took away a bad touch, but I did not give you a good touch, and you misinterpreted the absence of bad feelings as somehow feeling good.

Happiness is an emotion that tells us that a particular experience is a good thing, and we should do all we can to capture that experience or recreate it in the future. For example, you go on vacation to the Bahamas. The beaches are beautiful, the sun is dazzling, and the night air is peaceful. You hate for it to end, so you moan when you think about having to return home. Toward the end of the vacation, you may even consider extending your stay one more day. Then upon your return home, you start making your plans to return to the Bahamas next year. *This is the purpose of happiness.* It tells you that vacationing is enjoyable, and this particular vacation is so good that you should hang on to it a little bit longer or try to do it again. Happiness compels you to follow through and take action to capture the moment or recreate it.

Sadness

This is an emotion that we avoid, but it has a very important purpose. Sadness tells you that something important is missing. It causes you to shut out the world, turn inward, and reflect. Sadness is urging you to think about the important thing that is missing so that you can honor its absence and/or replace it in your life.

Consider the passing of my grandmother. Naturally, I was sad, but why? Grandma was not a particularly enjoyable woman. She was old, unattractive, and told the same unfunny jokes for years, but when she passed, I was very sad. Why? Because *Grandma was home.* She represented stability and family. It did not matter where I or my family lived or what was happening in the world. Grandma's house was always there. Every Thanksgiving, every Christmas, the entire family would gather at Grandma's, and we were all connected. We belonged.

When she passed away, my family began to realize it was important for everyone to be united, and so they established an annual family reunion to celebrate those who have passed on and to rekindle old connections to each other and to the past. They used their sadness to bring about the family connections that were important to them.

ANGER MANAGEMENT:

Fear

Fear's purpose is self-defense. When you spy a threat in your midst, the brain prepares the body to act quickly, and your mental focus is narrowed down to three basic thoughts: threat, fight, flight (sometimes freeze). Your attention becomes focused on the threat, and you are compelled to act to defend yourself.

Your body is prepared to help you perform your best in this situation. Your muscles tense so you can spring like a cat. Your heart beats faster to move oxygenated blood to the muscles you are about to use. Adrenaline begins to flow to give you additional energy, and the liver pumps out as much sugar as possible for more energy. You begin to sweat so your body will be cooled off like a radiator cools down your car's engine. Also, your mental focus narrows so that all you can think of is the thing threatening you. In the blink of an eye, your body goes from zero to sixty, your mind narrows your attention onto the threat, and all other thoughts are set aside, except for a couple of choice defensive options—fight or flight.

Most of us have seen home videos on television or YouTube in which an unsuspecting person is calmly walking along when someone jumps out in a gorilla suit. The person walking instantly reacts by becoming wide-eyed, flailing their arms about and running away. We all have a good laugh at how crazy they look.

Fear is a very good emotion for survival, but just try and imagine life without it. One morning, you step out of your house to find a vicious large snarling dog standing ten feet away. You have no fear to alert you to danger, narrow your mental focus, or charge up your body to respond quickly. Imagine all the logical evaluations and decisions you would have to make. "Hmm, large dog, snarling. This is a threat. Now what should I do? I could wrestle with him. No, probably not a good choice. Or I could try to run around him to my car, but he is probably quicker than me. Perhaps I could step back inside my house."

Before you could finish saying, "Hmm," you would have been mauled.

Anger

There are many other emotions, and we will discuss some of them in more depth later in the book, but as you see from the previous paragraphs, emotions have an important purpose. They are highly functional. So what about anger? The purpose of anger is to energize our bodies and focus our minds to *solve a problem*.

Think about it. Imagine you're paying your monthly bills. If you are like most of us, you probably dread sitting down and writing all those checks. Sometimes you hurry to get them done so you can go do other things.

As you sort through the bills, writing checks, you pick up the phone bill, and it is $32.76. As you are writing the check, you remember that last month's phone bill was different. You think, *Wasn't it something like thirty-three something?* You wonder why your phone bill fluctuates by pennies and occasionally a couple of dollars, but you finish writing the check and move on to the rest of the bills.

However, imagine that one month, you pick up that phone bill, and it is $176.14. *Screech!* Everything comes to a halt! You sit up straight (body becoming energized); eyes widen (to take in more light). You start trying to read all the itemized charges on the bill (mind is focused), looking for an explanation as to why the bill is unusually large. "Why is this bill so much?"

The other bills get pushed aside. Your plans for the evening are put on hold. Nothing else is going to happen tonight until this gets resolved. You grab your phone and call the phone company for an explanation. You may even stand up and pace. You endure the endless phone trees. "Press 1 for English."

"Push 7 if you would like to speak to a customer service representative."

"Please hold. All of our customer service representatives are busy now assisting other customers."

Your frustration rises even further.

Do you see what is happening? You have encountered a problem, and now your mind is focused on the threat (unusually large phone bill), and your body is energized to compel you to act and defend yourself against the threat. All other distractions are set aside so you can *solve this problem.*

When the bill was off by pennies, you had no emotional reaction. You just paid it. That is because there was no anger, so you were not emotionally compelled to do anything other than pay the bill. But when the bill was off by many dollars, the emotion rose up quickly and compelled you to act defensively. You were angry. You became energized and focused and called the phone company to straighten this situation out. *This is the purpose of anger.*

So what is the problem you are trying to solve? What is wrong with this picture? What needs to change? What is the threat? What do you do with this anger? All this and much more will be covered in the next chapter, which will lay out the details of the Anger Model.

Chapter 1 Study Questions

1. What is the purpose of emotions?

2. What does happiness do for us?

3. What does sadness do for us?

4. What is the purpose of anger?

5. Write about a specific time you were angry and did something you regretted.

ANGER MANAGEMENT:

6. In hindsight, what would you have done differently that would have been a better choice? In other words, what would you have been pleased with yourself for doing?

7. Begin to notice all of your emotions. Take a few moments throughout the day to turn inward and check out how you are feeling, even at times when you are not *feeling* anything. Maybe there is actually something there you just simply had not been noticing.

Chapter 2

The Anger Model

In the last chapter, we saw how emotions have a specific purpose. When we allow ourselves to actually *feel* our emotions and behave the way they compel us to, our lives are happier, more meaningful, and more productive.

Anger's purpose is to help us solve a problem. Anger gives us the energy and focus to deal with problems. But life is not a simple matter of paying bills. You have been in many situations that are much more complex, so let us look at a functional model of anger to better understand how anger actually works in our life.

To illustrate where the problem lies, let's look at an example of a typical angry interaction. This is one we have all encountered at some point in our life, hopefully not recently. First, look at figure A. This is how most people typically think of anger: (1) someone does something to you; (2) you become angry and do something back.

Keeping things simple for a moment, imagine someone calls you a name. What do you do? Retaliate by calling them a name, right? Makes sense. Well, at least we do it, but does it really make sense?

ANGER MANAGEMENT:

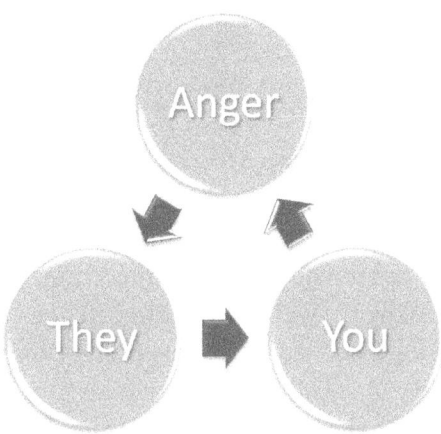

Figure A. Traditional Model of Anger

They call you a name and you call them a name back. Now ask yourself, "Why did I call them a name in return?"

Let's say they call you an *idiot!* You might respond with something equally insulting. Think about it a minute. Why are you calling them a name back? What were you hoping to accomplish? Before you read any further, think about the last time you did this and challenge yourself to answer *why* you called the other person a name after they just insulted you. Why did you call them a name? Write your answer in the space below.

_____

_____

When I ask students or clients, "Why do you call someone a name back when they call you a name?" there is always a long period of silence. They don't know why. They just do it. When I press for an answer, they start to answer with circular reasoning:

DR. PARKER: Tell me, why did you call them a name?
STUDENT: Because they called me a name!
DR. PARKER: I know. It is my example. But why did you call them a name *back*?
STUDENT: Because they called me a name first.

DR. PARKER: Okay, okay, different question. *Did it help?*

That last question is always a stunner. The most common answer I get is, "Help what?" See, as a psychologist, my job is to help you come to deal with life more effectively, so I am interested to know if what you are doing or not doing is helpful to you in accomplishing your life's ambitions. As a Christian, I know that God gave you talents and purpose, so I am also interested to know if your actions are helping you spiritually to fulfill God's purpose for your life.

Usually, if I keep the aforementioned questioning going, someone eventually says, "I called them a name back to show them what it feels like." Aha! But show them what feels like?

Look at figure A again. We agreed that this is how anger works. Now look at the model in figure A and identify what it is exactly you ware wanting the other person to feel. Anger? That is the only emotion that appears in figure A. They are obviously angry at you. They called you a name, so…you called them a name back to make them *angrier*? Does that make sense?

In the classes I teach, someone eventually shouts out, "To show them how much it hurts." Now we're getting somewhere. Hurt. But look at figure A again. Where does feeling *hurt* fit in that model? It doesn't. The rudimentary model we have been using in our daily life to understand anger is woefully incomplete. It is this incomplete understanding of anger that gets us into trouble and referred to an Anger Management class like this one. Anger is much more complex than we typically realize. Now let's look at figure B.

ANGER MANAGEMENT:

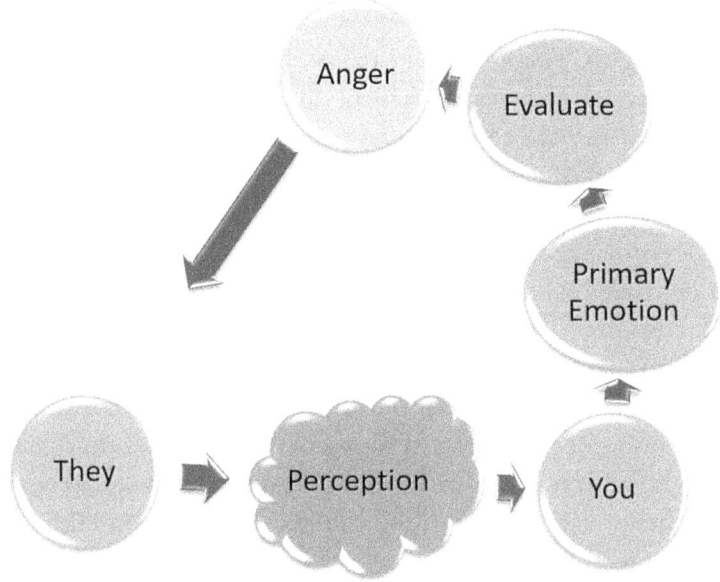

Figure B. The Anger Model

As you can see in figure B, the Anger Model is somewhat more complex, and there are two levels of emotional experience instead of just one. Primary Emotions and Anger. Notice, anger comes *second* in this model, so let's break it down and walk through this model using our simple example of name-calling. Once you understand the model at a simple level, you can start applying it to more complex issues.

Now let's take a deeper dive into each of the bubbles above.

Perception

Right off the bat, you see a difference. In figure B, there is something between *They* and *You*. It is called Perception. This is the act of perceiving (*gaining knowledge through our senses*), so the first thing you have to understand is that they are not doing anything to you. They are doing something, and you are *perceiving* it. This is a very important distinction.

When they called you an *idiot*, they did not reach into your brain and press a certain button that made you angry. They didn't touch you at all. The most you can say they did *to you* is they tickled your eardrums. They spoke, which vibrated the air. That air vibration traveled across the room and caused your eardrum to vibrate. That is all they did *to you*. *You* did the rest. You (using your brain) processed those vibrations and formed them into words. You then gave the words meaning (in your mind) based on the context of your situation. Based on this meaning, you gave the words power.

For example, you and your wife go to a dinner party. As the two of you arrive and begin to socialize with other couples, you go to the beverage table to fix yourself a drink, and you decide to fix one for your wife as well. You return to your wife and hand her the drink you so thoughtfully prepared for her. She takes one sip, makes a sour face, then turns to you and says, "Oh, this is all wrong, you idiot!" How would you feel? Hurt? Devastated? Humiliated? Embarrassed? This would be a Primary Emotion. Anger comes later.

But imagine a different scenario. Imagine you are having dinner with your best friend. You're feeling rather good about the night, so when the check comes, you grab it and say, "I got this."

Your best friend looks at you with surprise and says, "Oh, this is all wrong, you idiot!"

Now how would you feel? Hurt? Devastated? Embarrassed? Highly doubtful. You would probably feel rather smug and cocky and have a big grin from ear to ear. Why the difference? The words are exactly the same—"you idiot."

So why feel hurt in the first example and smug in the second? Because of your perception. The words are exactly the same. They both *did the same thing to you*. They vibrated the air and tickled your eardrums the same way. But your perceptions of the appropriateness of the words differ. When you are out with your wife, you think, *She shouldn't embarrass me like that. She shouldn't complain when I do something nice. She should have appreciated the gesture. She shouldn't speak to me like that in front of other people.*

But when you are out with your friend, and you steal the dinner check, you think, *He should protest.* You knew he would before you grabbed the check. In fact, if he didn't protest, you might get upset at him and never grab the check again. Besides, you know he doesn't really think you are an idiot. His smile and tone of voice communicated a different feeling. He is just upset you are paying for him and not letting him pay.

In the example with your wife, you perceive she does think you're an idiot and are deserving of a public tongue-lashing. This violates your basic beliefs of how to treat other people and shows great disrespect. Worse, she is totally ignoring the fact you tried to do something nice. Thus, your hurt emotions are in response to your *perception* of the situation, but they are not *caused* by the situation.

To further illustrate the role of perceptions, imagine a different scenario. You call your spouse, and they do not answer. You leave a voicemail, "Hey, sweetie, just calling to say hi and see how your day is going! Call me back!"

Thirty minutes pass, then an hour, and still no return call. Two hours. You start to get angry. Why? I love asking this question in the Anger Management classes because I get some pretty colorful answers! Below are just a few of the ones fit for reprint:

> She should've answered the phone when you called instead of ignoring you. (rejection)
>
> He should have at least called you back! (disrespect)
>
> She's not answering the phone or calling back? Why? What's she trying to hide!? (deception, paranoia)

Look at figure B again. What did *they* do to you? Literally nothing. You dialed her number. You spoke into the voicemail system. Your phone has not rung for two hours. Now look at some of the reasons people get angry. They may *think* they are being rejected or disrespected, or they may *think* their spouse is being deceptive and hiding an affair. But what are the *facts*, and what is your *perception*?

Facts: You left a voicemail. Your phone has not rung.

Perceptions: You are being rejected. You are being disrespected. You are being betrayed.

What are the *facts* about their behavior? Their thoughts? What do you know they did for a *fact*? Nothing. The only fact you have to work with is *your phone has not rung*. Depending on your perceptions, you will feel a variety of different Primary Emotions. If you perceive your spouse is ignoring you, then you may feel rejected or unloved. If you perceive your spouse is disrespecting you, then you may feel disrespected or unimportant. If you perceive your spouse is lying to you, you may feel betrayed or abandoned.

But all these emotions rely on *your* perceptions. All three of the above perceptions are possible, but do we have the facts to support the perception? What do we know for a fact? The phone has not rung for two hours. Other than the three possibilities above, what else could be happening to cause your phone not to ring for two hours?

1. Your phone is not working.
2. Her phone is not working.
3. The cell phone company is having technical difficulties.
4. One or both of you are in a bad cell area.
5. You did not pay the bill.
6. She was in an auto accident and can't call because she is injured.
7. He went into a store and left the phone in his car.
8. She is getting her hair cut and can't hear her phone in her purse.
9. He left the phone at home today.
10. _____

You *must* recognize that you are feeling an emotion based on your *perception* of the situation. The situation is not *causing* you to feel something.

ANGER MANAGEMENT:

You

Your perception of what they said *to you* gave the words meaning and power. However, if you perceive they were talking to someone else, you may not give the words the same meaning and power as if they were speaking to you. Consider a time when someone was mad and yelling, "Idiot!" But you thought they were speaking to the person standing next to you. In that instance, you felt fine. But when they clarified they were actually talking to you, not the other person, everything suddenly changed. The moment you realized their words were being directed at *you*, you began to have an emotional reaction.

Primary emotion

Before you get angry, you feel a Primary Emotion. Someone calls you a name. Your perception is that your wife is rejecting you. Now you feel a Primary Emotion. Hurt, rejection, unloved, used, discarded, threatened—the list goes on and on. It is very important to understand what your Primary Emotion is because this is the reason you are angry, and this emotion will guide all our future actions in the Anger Model.

Evaluation

This is a very short stage, but I point it out, nonetheless. (I like to call this stage, *Really?* We will come back to this later in the book.) At this stage, you evaluate what has gone on just before and decide if it is right or fair. They called you a name, and your perceptions led you to feel a negative primary emotion.

If in the Evaluation stage you reach the conclusion that what has transpired is "not right" or "not fair," you will become angry. Back to the example, your wife calls you a name. You perceive that she thinks you are stupid, and you find her tone belittling. This hurts. You feel rejected and humiliated. Now you evaluate this transaction. "I don't deserve this. This isn't fair." This conclusion is what ushers in anger.

If, for whatever reason, you decided it was fair, then you would not be angry. If, for example, as she was calling you a name, you remembered that she just told you, "Do not bring me a drink. I don't want to ruin my lipstick" You might think, *That's fair. She did tell me to not bring her a drink, and I did anyway.* But in this case, you decided it wasn't fair, so now…you become angry.

Anger

Now you are angry. Remember, anger is nothing but energy and focus, so the only question is, "What do I do with all this energy and focus?" If you try and bottle it up, you will explode. If you unleash it at the other person, you will be wasting the energy because you can't control other people. This is a key point that will be discussed later, but for now, understand that if your actions are aimed at changing what another person thinks, does, or feels, you are setting yourself up for more frustration and are giving control of yourself to them.

The key lies in focusing all of your energy and thoughts on what *you* have control over. When you do this, when you direct your God-given energy and focus on what you have power over, you do not feel *anger*. You are no longer judged as *angry*. Instead, you become *self-controlled*. You feel focused, motivated, driven, and determined. You now have the power to care for yourself and your family and the ability to make effective changes to life.

A step-by-step guide of how to apply this model to all situations will be covered later. First, you need a better understanding of some basic psychological concepts. The following chapters will discuss the importance of Boundaries, Perceptions, Emotional Well-Being, Assertiveness, and Listening. With these skill sets in place, you will be able to apply the whole model to various situations and manage your life with discipline and control.

A word about homework

You may have noticed already that at the end of each chapter are study questions. These questions are included for the casual reader as well as those participating in a formal class. The instructor can use the questions to stimulate discussion in class and assign the study questions as homework to be completed before the next class. But whether you're reading this on your own or studying in a classroom, it is necessary to complete the study questions. It is a very difficult process to take knowledge from a book and begin to actually apply it in real life on a daily basis.

The study questions are designed with two purposes in mind. First, it is a measure for the reader to determine if they gleaned the important concepts from the chapter. Secondly, the homework provides ideas about how to take the concept just discussed in the chapter and apply it in your daily life. When the homework is combined with good study habits, there is a better chance that you will be able to begin to make some subtle-but-meaningful changes in your life, so here is some homework to benefit you.

Chapter 2 Study Questions

1. What is the purpose of anger?

2. When you are angry, what is the problem you are trying to solve?

3. What is so important about understanding our perceptions?

4. Why do we need to be able to identify our emotions?

5. As the week unfolds, notice when you are becoming frustrated and angry. Each time you feel frustration or anger, write down what occurred and try to identify the Primary Emotion that preceded the anger (e.g., fear, hurt, rejection, disrespect, feeling unloved, betrayal, feeling ignored, etc.).

Chapter 3

Boundaries

This book is about you. Nothing in this book is to be misconstrued as a way to get others to do what you want or make them feel differently than they do. This book is about improving *your* life, not changing others. If you are truly prepared to change, then you will have to focus on yourself. You can't control other people (for a more in-depth discussion of this concept, refer to *Twelve Two: How to Transform Your Mind*).

When I say this in front of an audience, I get many nods of knowing. I am not surprised to hear someone mutter, "Amen." You have said it. You may have even said it to other people, but you don't practice it. You still tell other people what they should be doing, and you get very upset when they don't do what you think they should. Your wife should be more loving, and you tell her so. You complain because your kids won't do what their supposed to do. You get so frustrated when the bank won't waive the overdraft fee. You even try to control what others think. That bank manager—if he only understood it wasn't your fault. The bank didn't credit your paycheck deposit in time to cover your purchase at the store. You thought you had money in the account when you made the purchase. But he just refuses to listen. He won't even try to understand.

You even try to control how others feel. Yes, you do. Have you ever got even with someone? Why? To show them what it *feels* like. If they experience the same thing that they put you through, then maybe they will think twice before doing it again. They call you a name, and you call them a name back. Have you ever heard yourself say, "Don't like how it feels, do you?" But now, like a robot, you say, "I can't control anyone else." But you don't practice what you preach, and you have spent most of your life trying to control other people.

Truth: *you can't make others do anything, think anything, or feel anything*. Consider all the times you have tried, though. Maybe you have been after your fourteen-year-old son to clean his room. You asked, told, demanded, pleaded, threatened, screamed, and threatened some more. Maybe your wife left you or a girlfriend broke up with you. How successful were you at making her stay?

How many times have you explained yourself over and over and over, and they just don't get it? Frustrated, you tell yourself, "If they only understood, then they would change." But they just don't get it, and you become more frustrated with their ignorance and stupidity.

Have you ever tried to make someone love you? How successful were you? How about respect you? I am working with a gentleman right now who is forty-two years old, and he is still trying to make his father feel proud. Can't do it. Lord knows he has tried. Football star, college graduate, six-figure income, but every time he presents another success to his dad, his dad finds something to criticize, that is if he notices at all. Today, this successful big man sits across from me, frustrated, broken. He can't *make* his father feel proud of him.

Intimidation

Some people insist they can control others. Some men tell me, "They do what I say, or else!" Some women too. They use intimidation, and maybe it works—maybe once, maybe twice—but how long does that last? And if intimidation is such an effective technique, why doesn't it work on everyone? Why don't you use it all the time? Go into a convenience store and intimidate the cashier into giving you that soda and candy bar for free. Use intimidation on your boss to get your raise.

I'm not kidding. If you are going to tell me that you can make others do what you want through intimidation, then don't be scared to use it all the time. Think how much happier your life would be if you got what you want all the time.

But wait a minute. How do people act when you're not there to intimidate them? Your kids say, "Yes, sir," and "No, sir," in your presence, but do they say it when you're away? Employees work hard when the boss is standing over them, but how hard do they work when the boss leaves the jobsite? How about you? Do you obey the speed limit all the time, or just when you think the police are around?

Manipulation

Manipulation is another way people like to think they can control others, but is manipulation control, or is it simply creating an illusion that something good will result if they do what you want? When the saleslady laughs at your jokes, tells you how good you look in that sport jacket, and secretly reveals she thinks men with gray hair are sexy, are you more or less likely to buy the jacket? Are you buying the jacket because it is really a good deal or because she manipulated you by giving the illusion that she likes you and might even go out with you?

Intimidation and manipulation are coercion, not control. It is exactly because you can't control others that you have to resort to intimidation and manipulation to get someone to do what you want. If they were left to choose on their own, they probably would choose to do what they wanted, and that may or may not be what you wanted.

You can't control other people. You have to accept this premise to have any success in life. Think about it. I mean truly think about it. If we could control other people, would our jails be full? Would our drug rehab centers have waiting lists? If there was a way to control other people, don't you think some corporation would have patented it by now?

People come to me all the time and ask me to help them learn how to control their children, spouses, or themselves.

> My son won't stop hitting other kids. Can you make him stop?

> Doc, what do I do to get my husband to just listen to me for five minutes?

> Can you make me stop drinking?

I see it in their eyes. They want me to make them feel happy, make their pain go away, fix their kids, fix their husbands. Believe me, if I could control others, I would be charging $50,000 a visit. I picked up my first book on psychology in 1989, and I have been studying human behavior and change ever since. I will be the first one to stand up and tell you, "I can't control anyone." And if I can't, you certainly can't. Say it out loud, "I can't control other people!"

Now that you are accepting this, it is time to blow your mind. If you can't control other people, if you can't make them do anything, if you can't make them think a certain way, if you can't make them feel what you want, then you have to accept the logical flip side of that statement: *they can't control you.* If you can't control them, they can't control you. That means what you do, what you think, and yes, what you feel are completely under *your control.*

Now as I say this, many people start to feel dejected and even frustrated. "What you're telling me is if I am depressed, it is my own fault? If I am angry because they fired me for no good reason, I am somehow choosing to be angry, and I should just be happy about it?" Yes. Well, yes and no. Take the sarcastic comments out and then *yes.* If you are depressed, you are choosing to feel depressed. If you are angry, you are choosing to feel angry.

So again, extend the logic out. If you are creating misery, you can create peace. If you are creating depression, you can create happiness. If you are creating anger, you can create calm. If you can create negative emotions, you can create positive emotions. Only you control you, so focus on self-control. Remember, you can't control others, so they can't control you. So if they are not making you feel certain emotions, you *must* be creating them, and if you are creating these emotions in yourself, you can create any emotion you want. You just have to learn how. A deeper discussion regarding this is in

Twelve Two: How to Transform Your Mind. For this book, we will focus on how this concept applies to anger.

So the question becomes, how do I create different emotions? Well, changing your emotions is difficult, if not impossible. Go ahead and try…right now. Feel happy! Did you do it? No? How about… proud. Feel proud right now! Nope? That's right. It is extremely difficult to change an emotion directly, so we focus on the things we have direct control over—our thoughts and our behavior.

The basic you

In figure C, you see the core essence of yourself. You are comprised of Thoughts, Feelings, and Behaviors, and they are all interconnected. Different thoughts change how we feel, and different feelings change how we think. And different behaviors change how we think and feel. How we feel impacts what we do and so on.

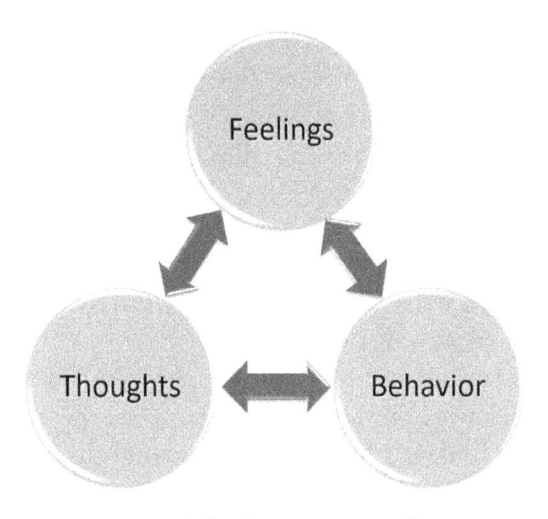

Figure C. The Core Essence of You

If you think negative thoughts about yourself and conclude the situation is hopeless, you may begin to feel depressed. Since you think the situation is hopeless and you feel depressed, you are now motivated to behave by quitting or trying only half-heartedly.

But the cycle can work the other way. If you think positively and conclude there is a chance, you may begin to feel better. Now that you feel better and think there is a chance, you are now motivated to behave by giving good effort.

This book is going to focus on you, not others. If you are going to feel better, if you are going to use your anger wisely and effectively, you have to focus on those things in life that *you* control—what you think, feel, and do. As you learn to understand how you think and how to change your thoughts, you will develop more control over how you feel. As you begin to understand your emotions and what their purpose is, you will begin to develop more realistic goals. As this occurs, you will begin to understand how to interact with others in an effective, rewarding manner, and anger will become your ally, not your enemy.

Many whom I deal with in my practice are in recovery from drug and alcohol addiction. As part of their recovery, they recite the Serenity Prayer at the end of most groups or meetings. When working with someone in recovery, and the topic of psychotherapy is anger, I will ask them, "What does the Serenity Prayer mean to you?"

They oftentimes think about it and have no real response. They usually recite it for me again as the definition of what it means. "Uh, it means grant me the courage to accept the things I cannot change…"

The typical response is, "It means I gotta let go. I know what you're telling me, but I can't just let go all the time! You're saying I should just let them walk all over me?"

We could spend weeks on this one sentence, but this is typical. They focus on letting go of something they can't control, and to most people, it sounds like a command. But listen to the Serenity Prayer.

Serenity Prayer

God grant me the Serenity to accept the things I cannot change,
The courage to change the things I can,
And the wisdom to know the difference.
—Reinhold Niebuhr

First, there is no demand in the prayer that you "got to let go." In the prayer, we ask God to grant us *serenity*. The serenity allows us to understand and accept that there are things in this world that we have no power over.

But there are two more lines in this prayer that are too often ignored. In the second line of the prayer, we request *courage* from God, courage to do, in many cases, what we already know to do. It may seem hard or scary, so that is precisely why we ask God to give us the courage to do it.

And finally, we request *wisdom*. We need wisdom to discern his will for our lives and specifically, this moment. We need wisdom to discern between what I cannot change and what I can. In other words, we ask for wisdom to see what we can control so we know exactly where to direct our mental focus and energy to create positive change.

Imagine that you have a serious legal matter, so you have set an appointment with the best attorney in town. You have taken time off from work to meet with him, and you know it will cost you a lot of money. The matter is serious, and you have been losing sleep over it. You lay awake at night rehearsing what you would say to the attorney so that you can get the most out of the meeting.

Finally, the day comes, and you hurry to the appointment. The receptionist ushers you into his office, and after polite introductions, you launch into your legal problem, but the attorney is not listening. He appears rather anxious, and he keeps glancing toward the window.

Finally, he interrupts you and asks, "Was it raining when you drove in?"

You tell him *no* and continue to lay out your problem, but he continues to glance out the window. He interrupts again and says, "Are you sure it wasn't raining?"

Now you're getting a little irritated. You are paying this man good money to help you, but he is not paying attention. Instead, he is worried about rain! He gets up and walks to the window and looks out and begins muttering about the weather. He is looking at the clouds in the distance and recalling the weather forecast on the news that morning.

He turns to you and says, "I'm sorry. I know I am supposed to be helping you, but I am so worried about the weather. You see, the weatherman said there was a fifty-percent chance of rain today, and I left my car window down. I hate it when my car seats get wet. The car really begins to stink, and it could ruin the interior."

He returns to his chair and shakes it off. "I apologize. I am supposed to be helping you. Please continue with your case." But as you begin to tell your story again, you see his eyes dart toward the window a couple of times.

Take a moment and think about this scenario. Imagine you are the client. At some point, what are you going to say to the attorney?

_____

_____

Most people tell me that they would tell the attorney, "Go roll up your window, then come back so we can concentrate on my issue." And in that moment, they embody the Serenity Prayer. *God grant me the serenity to accept the things I cannot change.* We give no thought to trying to control the weather. We simply note it. "Hmm, it may rain." *The courage to change the things I can.* We immediately turn our attention to what we can do. "My window is down. I better go roll it up." This is the Serenity Prayer. You become powerful and effective in your life when you possess t*he wisdom to know the difference.*

I use this example often because it seems the best way to illustrate the concept. Now pay attention. Here is a shortcut to some *wisdom*. There are five things in this world you have no ability to control, five things that the sooner you can make them the "weather," the sooner you will be happier, powerful, effective, and more successful.

1. The past
2. The future
3. What other people think
4. What other people do
5. What other people feel

ANGER MANAGEMENT:

The past is written and cannot be altered. The future has not occurred yet. How are you going to change something that has not happened? And as we saw earlier, we cannot control what other people do, think, or feel. So what do you control?

1. The present
2. What you think
3. What you do
4. What you feel

In the model

Look at the Anger Model (figure B). When you understand the concept of Boundaries, you can see that if you are going to be successful, all of your energies need to be directed at the things you control, which starts at Perceptions. Anything to the left of that line, you do not control, so if you direct your Anger toward anything on the left side of Perception, you are wasting your God-given power (focus and energy). What is on the left side of the line? What *they* are thinking, feeling, and doing. Your energy and focus have to be directed toward the things you can actually change—simply put, what you think, feel, and do.

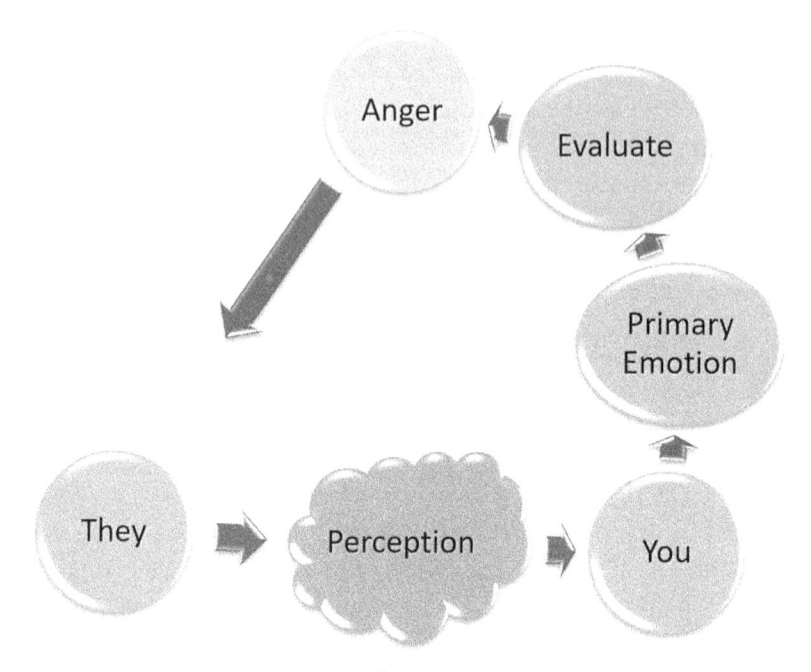

Figure B. The Anger Model

In the next chapter, we will begin focusing on how to change your thinking, not just *what* you think but *how* you think. Once you begin to think differently, you will begin to feel differently. As you begin to feel differently, you will begin to act differently.

ANGER MANAGEMENT:

Chapter 3 Study Questions

1. What four things do you control?

2. What five things are *not* under your control?

3. Think about a situation right now you are struggling with. Perhaps it is a disagreement with your spouse or frustration at work. Try to identify what it is specifically that you are upset about.

4. Focus on the situation you detailed in question 3. What about this situation do you *not* have control over? How is that related to your frustration?

5. What do you have control over in the situation?

6. Now focus on what it is you are *wanting* in the situation, not what *should* be but what you *want* (more about this in the next chapter).

7. What can you do, focusing only on the things you control, to increase the likelihood that what you *want* eventually occurs?

8. Begin to take the actions that you identified in question 7. After you take these actions, come back and write down how you felt when you began controlling what you actually can control.

Chapter 4

Perceptions—Should

This one word is solely responsible for a great deal of our depression, frustration, helplessness, hopelessness, and anger. Learning how to use this word appropriately can fundamentally alter your life.

Depression, frustration, annoyance, anger—these are experiences that we have of the world around us. We feel these emotions in response to events. As discussed earlier, all emotions have a purpose. Frustration signals that we are being prevented from achieving our goals, like when we are walking through a crowded store trying to shop, and people keep getting in our way. Annoyance tells us that something or someone is distracting us from what we are engaged in, like that guy in the office who keeps tapping his pen on his desk.

Depression tells us something important is missing. Maybe it is a purpose in life or the belief that things will ever get better. Maybe it is that future you had envisioned that gets ripped away when you lose your job, or your spouse falls ill. Maybe you're missing the confidence to go forward into a new chapter of life. Maybe your daily experiences are a series of pressures, frustration, annoyances, and little joy or happiness, and it is all beginning to take a toll on you. Depression is complicated and can come from many sources, but a large portion of depression comes from the word *should*. Anger, irritation, frustration definitely are the byproduct of *should* statements.

While we tend to view emotions as our experience of the world around us, this is not quite true. Our emotional experience is actually the product of our *perception* of the world around us. Haven't you ever noticed how some people love shopping, and others dread going to the mall? Or how the first snowfall of the year puts some people in a great mood while others get dark and sullen? Do you know someone who can walk into a room and immediately spot everything that is wrong?

What about you? Think about your day and what experiences are most common for you. When you wake up in the morning, do you have a list of things you must do that day? Do you check in with yourself periodically throughout the day to see if you have done all that you should? How do you feel at night if you didn't get it all done? A little guilty? Frustrated? Do you find that you use guilt and pressure to motivate yourself to do things? How do you feel when the cashier at the store does not smile and say, "Thank you?" How about when the car in front of you suddenly brakes and turns without having signaled his intention to do so with a turn signal? How do you feel? What is your dining experience like when the waiter is slow? Do you have any joy and happiness in your life? What do you look forward to?

Perceptions are part of how we think. They are mental filters that allow certain parts of reality through while blocking other parts from being noticed. Much like colored lenses in sunglasses will change how you *see* the world around you, mental perceptions change your *experience* of the world around you—in other words, how you feel about things.

ANGER MANAGEMENT:

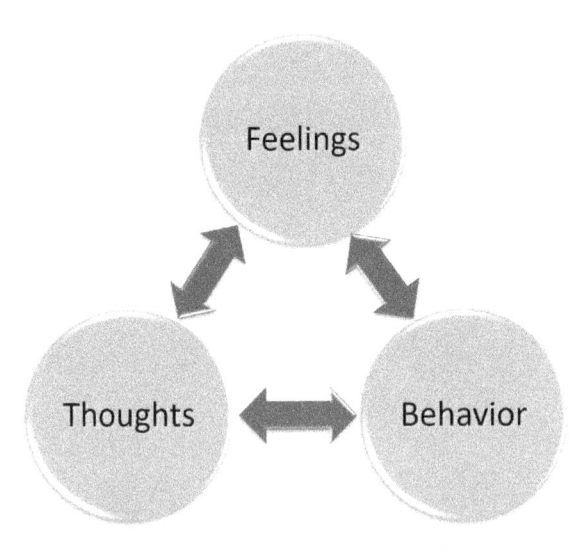

Figure C. The Core Essence of You

This is where *should* statements comes in. The word *should* is not a perception but a clue to the fact that you are viewing the world through a perceptual lens of *expectations*. Whenever you hear yourself saying or thinking *should, must, have to, need to, got to, supposed to*, you are in a mindset of expectations, and the more you're in this mindset, the more likely that you battle with frustration, anger, and depression. Filtering reality through a lens of expectations does three things to you. First, it only allows you to experience negative emotions. Secondly, it gives control of yourself to others. Third, it builds resentments.

Emotional experience

When you view the world through expectations, you have only two possible experiences 99 percent of the time. Either you will experience some form of frustration, irritation, anger, or guilt, or you will experience *nothing*. And rarely—maybe only 1 percent of the time—is it possible for you to experience something positive (see figure D).

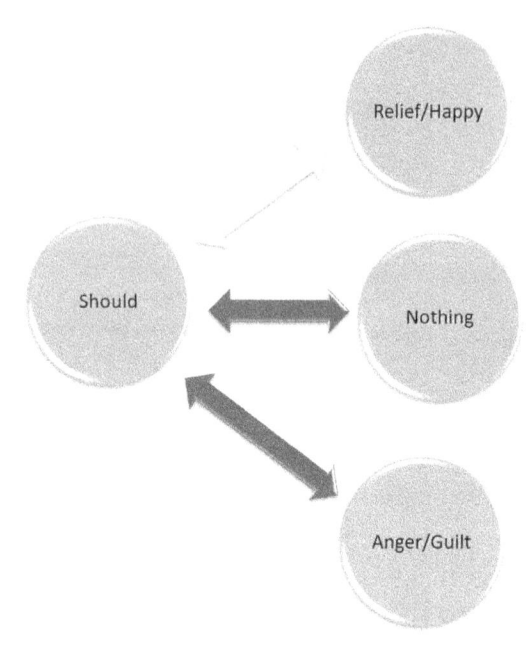

Figure D. Should Perspective

Let's break it down. How do you feel when others *don't do what they should?* Frustrated? Angry? When walking through a crowded store: "This guy in front of me *should* get out of my way!" If the waiter has not come to your table quick enough: "Where is the waiter? He *should've* been here by now!"

How do you feel when they *do what they should?* When I ask this question of people for the first time, they usually reply, "Happy," or "Good, I guess." But think about it. You really don't experience anything. Consider the above questions. You're in the store, and it is crowded. You're looking for a shirt. As you walk to the clothing department, you get stuck behind a couple of people talking and looking around as they walk. There is a stream of people going the opposite direction of you, so you can't really get around these two people. They walk at a normal pace then suddenly slow to look at the sales price on a purse hanging on a rack, but they don't step aside; they just slow down, see the price, and keep walking while talking.

Meanwhile, you're stuck behind them. Your frustration grows. Listen to what you are telling yourself even as you're reading this paragraph.

> They *should* speed up!
>
> They *should* be more considerate and let others walk by!
>
> They *should* step out of the aisle so they're not in everyone's way!

These are the *thoughts* that generate frustration and anger.

How would you feel if they did exactly what they *should*? If they walked faster or stepped out of the aisle to check out the hats so you could walk by? You would feel *absolutely nothing*. If they were walking faster, you would not have paid any attention to them. If they were walking at your pace, saw something they wanted to check out, and walked over to it, thus clearing the aisle, you would never even know that they were being considerate. Therefore, you would not have even noticed that they chose to walk quickly and get out of everyone's way when they decided to stop. And so your day goes. You notice people doing things they *shouldn't* and others not doing what they *should*. Your day becomes filled with more and more irritation, frustration, and anger.

Think about it. How many times have you complained the city *should* fix the potholes? But when have you felt happy because the street did not have a pothole? How many times have you complained about the driver in front of you who was driving slowly? But how many times did you feel a great sense of respect for all the drivers who did not impede your progress?

Now how about yourself? What do you feel when you don't do what you *should*? Some amount of pressure, self-loathing, and guilt are usually what's in store. Right now, I want you to think of something you *should* get done. Say it out loud. Now think about how you said it. Did you grit your teeth as you said it, nod your head yes, purse your lips together, groan? You beat yourself up for not doing all the things you *need to* do, *should* do, are *supposed to* do. You pressure yourself and feel guilty when you don't meet your own *expectations*. You whip yourself to get things done. You knuckle down, quit goofing off, and make yourself do everything right. You experience stress and pressure.

In figure D, you can see that once you say *should*, you have only two options, negative emotions or nothing. But occasionally, you do feel something akin to pleasant. Usually, it is after a *should* has not been met for quite some time. For example, you haven't kept up with your chores like you *should*. Your car is getting dirty, the dishes are piling up, and you haven't been to the gym in weeks. Maybe you have been drinking more than you *should*. You're feeling kind of guilty for neglecting things, and you're not happy with yourself. You've been staying out too late.

So you get on yourself. You tell yourself to "straighten up and fly right." You get the car cleaned up and the dishes done. You get your clothes all put away, you go for a run, and you go to bed on time. A feeling comes over you that you interpret as pleasant. You might even let out a satisfactory sigh. You got everything caught up, and you no longer feel bad about yourself. You're finally able to relax.

But think about it. Is this really a pleasant feeling, or is it just the absence of the pressure and guilt? Isn't that what relief is, the absence of something negative? Is that really all that wonderful? If I squeezed your fingers tightly for five minutes then let go and relieved the pressure, would you be happy with me? Certainly not, but we mistake relief for happiness all the time. We fall behind, whip ourselves into getting caught up, then we get a sense of relief, and we tell ourselves we're happy. Maybe your boss is always griping about something. It is a rare day he does not yell at someone. And on those rare days he is not yelling, are you actually happy he didn't yell, or are you just relieved you made it through the day and did not get in trouble?

There is the possibility to feel actual positive emotions after saying *should*, but it is rare. The only way to actually *feel* happiness, joy, pride, accomplishment when you're approaching the world through a lens of *should and expectations* is when you or others *exceed* your expectations. It is not enough that your wife cleans the house and cooks dinner every night. You notice it sometimes, but you don't feel loved and honored by her for these things. You don't feel special. In fact, you probably have to remind yourself to thank her for these things. You say, "Thank you," because you're *supposed to*.

No, for you to actually *feel* special and honored by your wife, she has to go over the top. The house has to be immaculate and smell nice when you walk in. The dinner she cooks has to be your favorite. The table has to be set nicely, and she has to break out the fine dishes. And she has to surprise you with all this. You walk in and see all this *unexpectedly* and say, "Wow! Honey, the house looks great, and the food smells delicious! This is wonderful!" You actually feel her love and honor, but your expectations had to be *exceeded* for this to occur.

Look at figure E for an illustration of how your day begins to shape up and which experiences get painted on your canvas of life. As you go along, you notice all the things that *others* are doing wrong.

> He should be doing this instead of that.
>
> Traffic should speed up.
>
> They should be more courteous.
>
> She should just leave a message instead of calling repeatedly.

You notice all the things *you* are doing wrong.

> I need to get all this done.
>
> I gotta start working out.
>
> I should have been nicer.
>
> I gotta remember to call like I keep promising.

But what about all the things *that go right?* The people who are courteous? The waiter who is timely? The things you did well? You don't really even notice most of these things, so they fade into the background and drop off your canvas, so you don't see or experience anything positive.

```
                    Frustration


                                        Upset

            Annoyance


                                Shock

    Shame


                        Guilt


        Self-loathing


                                    Anger




    Mad             Irritation
```

Figure E. Typical Experiences After Should Statements

The things that go right cannot be experienced because they are *supposed* to happen. So most of your experiences throughout the day and week are negative ones, and the longer this goes on, the more frustrated you feel and the greater the chance you can become angry or depressed because if this is what life is like, what is so great about living?

Should statements also give away your control. For example, a young lady may have an expectation of her boyfriend. "He should be a gentleman and open the door for me." How is she going to feel if he doesn't open the door? Rejected? Unloved? Unappreciated? Angry at him for not opening the door like he *should*?

How will she feel if he does open the door? She will *feel* nothing. If he is consistent, she won't even notice he does it every time. If he is inconsistent, then she is probably getting tense as she approaches the door, and she is starting to get angry in advance. She thinks, *Okay, here we are at the restaurant door. He better start walking ahead and reaching out for the door. I have told him a thousand times he should be a gentleman and open the door for me. He better not forget!* She is getting angry as she imagines him not doing what he *should*, so when he does do it, she will experience relief that he finally remembered.

But think about the fundamentals involved in her anger. If he doesn't open the door, she feels ignored and angry. If he does open the door, she doesn't feel anything. His actions determine her emotions. She has given control of herself to him.

Think about the fundamentals involved in feeling positive emotions. Others have to exceed your expectations for you to feel love, happiness, joy, or respect. It is not enough for the cashier to scan your products and take your money. In order for you to feel it was a good shopping experience, the cashier *has to* be friendly, pleasant, efficient, and speedy. So all of the experiences you are having are because of someone else's actions, and you are not in control of anything. If you're upset, it is someone else's fault, and in order for you to feel good, others have to exceed your expectations.

We discussed earlier that the truth is that only you control how you feel. But the reason it feels like others are controlling you is because you *give away* that control when you adopt a perceptual filter of *should, must, have to, gotta, supposed to, expect.*

Finally, *should* statements build resentments. It is simple math. Consider the young lady's expectation of her boyfriend. He doesn't open the door; she feels ignored and angry. Once this is done, the event is written in stone and cannot be changed. He can never go back in time and open the door. So every time she thinks about the past event, she will experience the exact same frustration with him. It does not matter if it occurred five seconds ago or five days ago. She will recall the moment he did not open the door for her, and she will feel ignored and angry. His offense (in her mind) will be added to the list of everything else he has done wrong that can never be changed. When does she get to stop feeling resentful? Never.

What to do

At this point, I usually start getting doubtful looks. You're probably getting the impression that I am telling you to not have any expectations. Wrong. Have expectations, but have *reasonable* expectations. Be *realistic*. Here is how. Whenever you hear yourself saying *should, must, have to, need to, gotta, supposed to,* or *expect*, stop yourself and ask the following questions:

Is it a law?

Can we put them in jail for that?

Can they be fired from their job?

Is this a reason to file for a divorce?

If the answer is *yes*, then you are being reasonable and realistic. Keep it as a *should* and handle it in the legally prescribed manner. Call the police; ask to speak to the manager. But if the answer is *no*, then change how you think. Change your perspective from *shoulds* to a *personal preference*. But if what you are saying *should* about is not a law where people are jailed or employees are fired or spouses are divorced, then it is not a reasonable *expectation*. It is something you are *wanting*, something you desire or prefer.

A *preference* is just as valid as an *expectation*. You are not settling or giving in; you are changing your perspective of the situation. You are changing how you think about the matter. You are adopting a more realistic perspective of the matter. You no longer have to experience guilt, frustration, and anger if it does not happen a certain way. But if things do go the way you want, you now will have the opportunity to actually experience something positive (figure F).

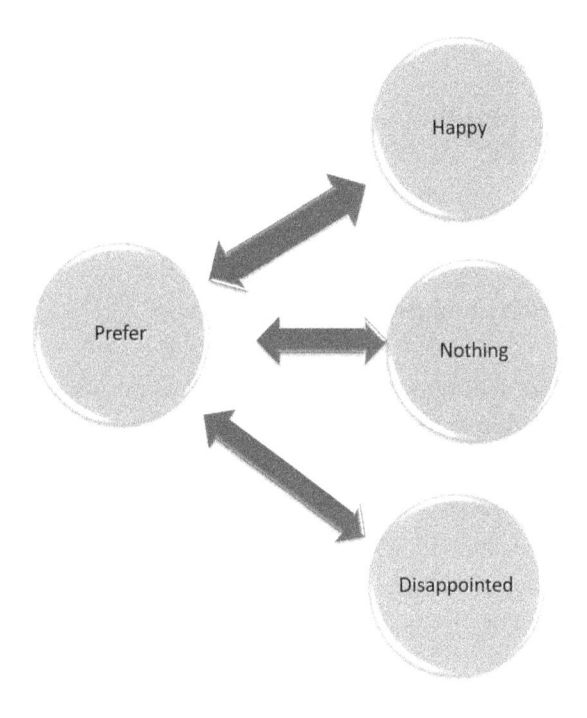

Figure E. Preference Perspective

Example of the young lady: "He *should* open the door." Possible outcomes:

1. He opens the door, she experiences nothing.
2. He doesn't open the door; she feels ignored and gets angry. She blames him for ruining her evening and remains angry at him for days. They argue over this, and she tells him he better start treating her nicer if he wants her to stick around. He feels pressure whenever they go out to never make a mistake.

She decides to challenge her *should* statement. *Is it a law?* "No. We don't throw people in jail for this, and it is probably not a reason to break up with someone, so the reality is this is a personal preference."

She rephrases her *should* statement in terms of what she would *like*. "I would like it if he held the door open for me. I would feel special if he did." Possible outcomes:

1. He opens the door for her, and she can now feel what she said she would—special. She is getting something she wants, so it feels good.
2. He does not open the door. She feels disappointed because she is not getting what she wants. But she doesn't feel frustration or anger.

This new emotional experience of disappointment allows her to see the situation differently and choose a different response. Later, she decides to change the things she can. Rather than focusing on what he *should* be doing (something she does not control), she focuses on her behavior and decides that she could tell him that she feels special when he opens the door for her. This is all she controls, so she puts her energy there. Because she chose to share with him what she is thinking and what she would like, he can begin to understand what is important to her and how she receives love. He now knows what to do if he wants to show her that she is special to him. He becomes motivated to open doors for her because he knows it will be received positively, and that is rewarding to him.

By applying reality to our expectations and challenging all of our *should* statements, we start to experience our reality in a more reasonable and realistic fashion.

Now there are *should* statements that are considered universally appropriate. They are usually a law of some form—for example, laws developed through legislation for criminal or civil circumstances. Company policies can be considered a form of law. The company may require employees to show up to work at a specified time or face termination. Then there are personal laws that we create. "My spouse should be 100 percent faithful, or I will divorce her." There are no legal laws against affairs in America (can't arrest them), and there are no civil laws either (can't sue them), but you may determine that an affair is a valid reason to terminate a marriage. That is your *law*.

Recognize, if you put a *should* on someone else, then you are actually putting a *should* on yourself as well. Therefore, if you conclude that what you are saying *should* about is a law based on one of the categories above, then respond by thinking how you are *supposed to* respond. What is the appropriate legal response?

- People *should* use a turn signal and drive the speed limit. They are violating a legal law. What is the appropriate legal response? Chase after them? Pull them over? Yell at them? No. You are *supposed to* pull your car over and make a police report.
- Waiters *should* serve you the dinner you ordered. If they don't, do you have a right to scream at them? Throw the plate on the floor? No. You are *supposed to* explain the misunderstanding. If the waiter cannot resolve your complaint, then you call for the manager. If the manager cannot provide a satisfactory outcome, you politely leave and write a letter to the restaurant owner.
- Your child *should* clean his room. This is not a legal or civil law, but it may be a parental law. If so, do you have a right to scream at them? No. When a child misbehaves, choose an appropriate parenting technique in response.

If you determine something is a *law*, then deal with it in the legally prescribed fashion. Use your energy and focus (anger) to follow through with the police or talk to the restaurant manager. Use your anger to focus on setting limits on *your* actions. "I said if your room was not clean by 5:00 p.m., you could not go to the movie. It is not clean, so you must stay home." Now follow through. Be resolute and determined. Do not try to control them. You can't, so pour your energy and focus into controlling yourself by consistently following through with the negative consequence the child has chosen by misbehaving.

But the real truth is most of life is a personal preference.

> I appreciate people being courteous, paying attention, and saying, "Thank you."

> I feel honored by my wife taking care of the house. It is not her job, and it is not a reason to divorce her if she doesn't.

> I feel a sense of pride and accomplishment when I keep my work caught up.

By rephrasing the sentence and shifting from *should* statements to *preferences*, I am actually restructuring my thoughts, reprogramming my brain, changing how I think. When I do this, I increase the opportunities for me to experience positive emotions. I take back control of my life rather than making others responsible for me, and I don't carry around resentments that festers and make me bitter.

"I should run more. Is this a law? No, but I feel really good when I run, so I would like to start running more."

Listen to your thoughts and constantly challenge them. Maybe you are driving down the highway, and someone is driving slow in the left lane. You may automatically think, *He* should *speed up if he is going to be in this lane!* This creates frustration, and maybe you begin tailgating him and flashing your lights. Now challenge that thought. Is this a law? Maybe, depending on your state, but what are you really wanting? *I would like to be able to drive fast, and it would be really nice if this driver would pull to the right and let me pass.* Now that you have changed your thinking, notice that your emotional experience changes as well, and new options rise to the surface for how to respond to the situation.

It is incredible how much of our life is ruled by *should* statements. People really feel terrible if their desk is cluttered or if their car is dusty. Is this reasonable? Is it so horrible to have dust on your car that you have to feel frustrated about it? And when the car is clean, do you truly feel happy? No. you feel *relieved* by the absence of the frustration brought on by the *should*. Relief is the absence of something bad, not the presence of something good. So all day long, you put pressure on yourself, create frustration, and then begin acting to relieve the frustration (you created). The best outcome is the *relief* from the self-generated frustration with no possibility of any positive feeling.

The more we think in terms of *should* statements, the more frustration, anger, and negative feelings we experience. The more we feel others are to blame, the more resentments we carry. The longer this goes on, the more likely we will experience depression, the more likely we will have problems in our relationships. We begin feeling like everything is going wrong, and it is everyone else's fault. This one word, *should*, is extremely powerful (and the substitutes: must, have to, need to, gotta, supposed to, expect, etc.).

The word itself is not bad, but it is a clue to how we are thinking, and this frame of mind, this cognitive distortion, puts us in a mindset where we will only be creating negative experiences. By getting this thought process under control, you will significantly change your life. You will see an immediate reduction in the amount of pressure, frustration, and anger you feel. You will take back control over your life and begin creating much more rewarding, positive experiences. Who knows, you may actually start to enjoy life!

In the model

Now look at the Anger Model. Locate the bubble for Perceptions. Notice they are the first component of the model. There is a reality of the actions of others, but it is only known by you after it comes through your perceptions. This is very important. They are doing things, but you are *perceiving* what they are doing.

Take the example of the wife not returning your phone call. You may say, "She is ignoring me or blowing me off," but what are the facts? Your phone has not rung. Anything beyond that is speculation based on *your perceptions*. You are thinking *should* statements. *She* should *answer my phone call. She* should've *called back by now. She* shouldn't *ignore me.* You are distorting the reality of the situation, which, in turn, creates the feelings of hurt, rejection, being ignored, being threatened, and it eventually leads to anger.

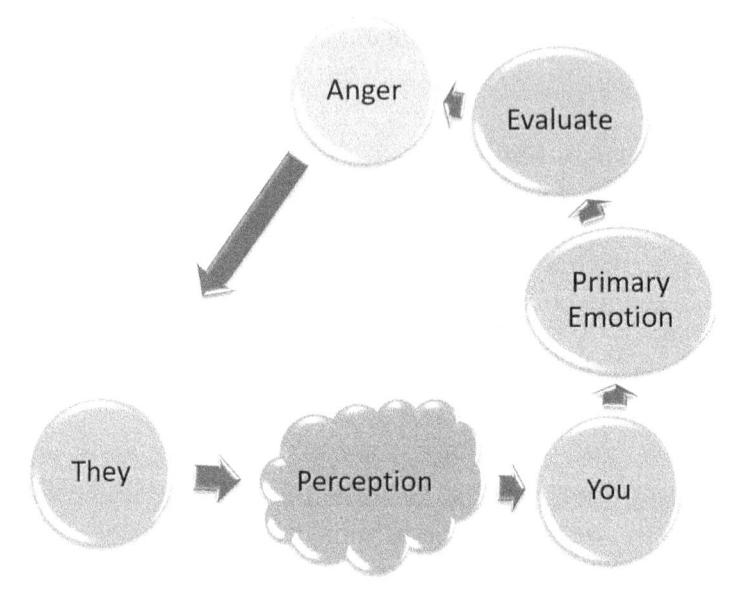

Figure B. The Anger Model

ANGER MANAGEMENT:

Chapter 4 Study Questions

1. Practice rephrasing *should* statements as preferences. Here are a few simple ones to try out. People *should not* use the drive-through lane to order lunch for the entire office. Is this a law? No. Now rewrite this thought in terms of a preference. Look back at the examples in the chapter if you need guidance. My family *should* keep their voices down when I am trying to watch the news.
2. Increase your awareness of how much of your life is ruled by expectations. For one day, carry a sheet of paper and count how many times you say or think *should, must, have to, need to, gotta, expect,* or *supposed to.*
3. On the second day, begin writing down the *should* statements. See what they look like when you read them on a sheet of paper.
4. On the third day, begin challenging the *should* statements. Each time you catch yourself saying *should, must, have to, need to, gotta, expect,* or *supposed to,* stop. Write it down and ask yourself, "Is it a *law*?" Can you call the police or have the person fired or file for divorce about the matter? If it is not a *law*, rephrase the *should* in terms of what you are wanting. What would you like? What do you want? How would you like things to be? What would you prefer? What benefit are you seeking from this situation? Write this down and then return to the situation or the thought. Evaluate how you feel after replacing the distorted thought (should) with the more reasonable or realistic thought (preference.) Do this exercise as often as possible for the next five days.
5. Beginning in week 2, leave the paper behind but continue to listen to yourself and catch yourself saying *should, must, have to, need to, gotta, expect,* or *supposed to.* Ask your spouse or a close friend to gently call it to your attention. Continue to rephrase the *should* statements in terms of what it is you are wanting or would like to have happen.
6. Notice, each time you say and think and visualize what it is you are *wanting*, you begin to see a pathway to achieving your desired outcomes. With practice, this new way of thinking becomes automatic, and you will begin focusing on your desires, goals, and dreams.

Chapter 5

Perceptions—Jumping to Conclusions

The perceptual process is very important in all that we do. That is why this book focuses so much attention on it. In the last chapter, I reviewed probably the most important way we distort our reality and create unnecessary stress, tension, and anger in our lives. In this chapter, I want to review a second cognitive distortion that is important to understand if you are going to use your anger effectively.

When we jump to conclusions, we are assuming things to be true that we do not know for a fact. That is a nice way of saying it. Another way, equally true, is *we are substituting fantasies for reality*. This is actually what you are doing, but it doesn't sound so harmless when it is put that way.

And we do this more than we might imagine. For example, an employee might say, "Oh, man, when I get to work, my supervisor is going to be in a bad mood and will make my day miserable."

A husband may think to himself, *Crud, she's complaining about a headache. I guess we won't be making love tonight.*

A grandparent may despair, "They only agreed to come over because they feel sorry for me. They really don't want to be here."

Fantasies

We have all thought or talked like this, but we must call it what it is. These are *fantasies*, not realities. Think about it. Answer these questions honestly. Can you predict the future? Can you read other people's minds? Because this is what you are attempting to do when you jump to conclusions. You read another person's mind, make a prediction about the future. Then you act as if the *fantasy* you just imagined is really what they were thinking or is truly what will happen. When you *fantasize* about things you can't possibly know for a fact (others' thoughts, the future), you have just jumped to a conclusion.

What is funny about this is that while people will agree with me, they will turn around and defend themselves for doing it. It is like they are saying, "Yeah, I know I can't predict the future or read their mind, but I am usually pretty good at it, so let me keep doing it."

Self-fulfilling prophecy

One of the reasons we *think* we are good at predicting the future is because of something called the Self-Fulfilling Prophecy. This is a phenomenon in which you actually create the future that you predict. And since the future you predicted came true, you erroneously reason you must have the power to predict the future. This circular reasoning increases the likelihood that you will jump to more conclusions in the future.

For example, a client once came to me depressed and out of work. He was college educated, and for three years after college, he was the assistant manager of a department store. However, he lost that job and fell into a depression. He moved in with his mother and was unemployed for four years. Now he was trying to get his life back together and get back into the workforce. He enrolled in therapy and submitted applications to seven different large department stores around town.

One afternoon, he came to therapy, fell into the chair, and hung his head. He looked like he was feeling down, dejected, maybe depressed. I asked, "What's wrong?"

He replied in a sullen voice, "Bullseye Department Store called me in for an interview."

I was confused. This sounded like good news (remember, we are dealing with perceptions here). I remarked, "And this is bad news because…?"

He explained, "Sorry, I didn't explain. They called me in to interview for the position of manager. I applied to be an *assistant* manager."

Still confused, I said, "And that is bad news because…?"

He mustered up some frustrated energy and said, "Look, you don't understand how it works. In the world of big business, you can't just hire your friend. You're not allowed to do that, so if you want to hire your friend, you have to pretend to hold job interviews. In that case, you call people in for interviews who are *not* qualified for the job. After you interview everyone, you can then claim that your friend was the best qualified person for the job!" He sank back into his chair. "They are just using me. I'm not going to get the job, and it will be a big waste of my time. For what? So some jerk can hire his buddy?" As he finished explaining, he grew angrier and more helpless and more depressed.

This was a tough position for me. His job interview was the next day. Normal therapy might take months to help him understand his self-defeating thoughts. If I simply told him what he was doing to himself, he still might not have time to pull out of the tailspin before the interview or, worse yet, simply add that to his list of failures, so I chose to manipulate the circumstances a bit. I mused out loud with him, "Well, look at it this way: you never really wanted to work at Bullseye, did you?"

He said, "No."

I reminded him, "You were hoping to get on with Stuff Mart, right?"

He muttered, "Yeah."

I pretended to think out loud, "Hmm, when was your last actual job interview? Seven years ago? That's a long time. And job interviews are a lot more complex than we usually realize. I mean, you gotta have your clothes ironed and ready to go. You have to have your resume up to date, and you have to get out of the house and to the interview without spilling coffee all over your shirt. Then once you get there, you have to answer silly questions and try and impress people. That is a lot to do."

He seemed to become more depressed as I spoke and slowly sighed, "Yeah."

I then said, "Well, what about this? Instead of letting them use you, why don't *you* use Bullseye?"

He looked at me confused.

I explained, "Well, you know you're not going to get the job, so there is no pressure, right? Besides, you really didn't want to work there, but you have not been to a job interview in *seven* years! So *use* them like they were going to use you. This is a chance for you to practice your job interview skills. It is a free dry run. It doesn't matter if you make a mistake because you're not getting the job anyway, right? So use this opportunity to prepare for the job interview you really wanted! Get dressed up. Go to the interview. Tell jokes. Take the opportunity to hear what silly questions they ask so you can come up with good answers for the real interview. Heck! Do something silly just to get it out of your system so when you go to the real job interview, you are composed, confident, assured, and prepared!"

As I laid out this idea, he slowly brightened. By the time I finished, he was sitting up straight and smiling. "Yeah! I'm going to use them!"

We ended the session, and he left very excited.

The next week, he came in and had a sheepish grin on his face. I asked, "What's going on?"

He smiled and said, "I went to the interview at Bullseye without a care in the world. Shoot, I was even flirting with the receptionist. They were late for the appointment, but I really didn't care. When he finally called me in, I told jokes and had us both laughing. I made up some BS to those stupid interview questions, and in the middle of it, we were interrupted because of some big 'emergency' out on the floor.

"The guy interviewing me excused himself to go see what the problem was, and I tagged along. They had an issue with a floor display, and they were making a big deal out of nothing, so I finally told them, 'Why don't you just do this, and that will fix it.'

"They looked at me like I was some sort of genius! The guy offered me the job of manager right on the spot!"

Do you see what happened? Think about it a minute. If he had gone to the job interview with his original attitude ("They are using me. There is no chance I will get the job"), how would he have performed? How much effort would he have given? What kind of mood would he have been in? How would he have answered their questions? What would he have done when the interviewer had to leave the office to oversee the emergency? And most importantly, would he have been offered the job?

The answers are obvious. He would have been in a bad mood, gave short answers, and sat in the office brooding when the interviewer left. The result would have been he would not have been offered the job, like he had predicted.

What to do

One might think that I am saying, "Don't worry." That is not the case at all. What I am saying is think effectively. Worry is not effective. It is a waste of energy and creates nothing but stress, tension, pressure, fear, and depression. It is unproductive. You think, *Oh my gosh! What if* _____ [fill in the blank]? It doesn't matter what follows because you are now in worry mode, so you are going to be ineffective. You can choose to think in a different way. Adopt a different perspective about the future or what others may think.

Besides, telling yourself to *not* do something is the worst thing you can do. Try this simple experiment. Look around the room and pick out an object, maybe a vase. Now look straight ahead and tell yourself, "Don't look at the vase. Just don't think about it." What happened?

Most people report that the vase begins to glow like a light bulb. They find they start physically straining to not notice the vase, and they sometimes have to actually turn their head away. Now here is what I want you to really notice. The vase has been there *the entire time*, and all this time, you have not been thinking about it…effortlessly. It was not until you told yourself not to look at it or think about it that you had to exert any energy to put it out of your mind.

Now that was just a vase. Imagine how much energy you have to exert to put something of real value out of your mind. Thus, when we tell ourselves, "Don't worry," because we don't want to stress about it, we are actually *magnifying* our stress in our attempts to feel less stress.

Realize, once you say, "What if...?" the nightmare appears in your mind. Your brain will process that mental image that you just imagined in much the same way it would as if you were really seeing it unfold in front of you. Basically, from a mental and physiological standpoint, when you worry, you are experiencing the same stress as if the worry was really happening. You begin to get stressed or anxious, and you start to develop tunnel vision. You lose the ability to think clearly and move into fight-or-flight mode.

Instead of worrying, rephrase the worry from a *what if* to a *concern*. Literally rephrase the sentence and say, "I am concerned that...," and add the *concern* to the end of the sentence. What this does for you is move the image out of your face and places it at arm's length. It gives you breathing room. It helps you understand that this isn't happening right now, but it is a *possibility*.

So if it is possible that this event could occur, then plan for it. What would you do if this event came to pass? You have a plan for flat tires, so make a plan for this.

Now recognize that your concern is only a *possibility*, one possible outcome out of many. That means there are other *possibilities*, so which of the other possibilities would you prefer to see happen? Once you identify your preferred future, begin making a plan to increase the likelihood that future actually occurs.

For example, let's say you are worried that your husband might get mad when he learns that you drove over his favorite golf club. You worry, "Oh my god! What is he going to say? What is he going to do? What if he yells at me? He won't even listen to me and let me explain it's his fault for leaving it out. I will start crying again, and he will call me a baby like usual. I can't stand it when we argue like that." You can hear the defeat and anger, and the actual conversation has not yet occurred.

Instead, say to yourself, "I am concerned he will become angry and yell when he learns about his golf club." Now create a plan to deal with that possible concern. "Well, if he begins yelling, I can wait for him to get done, or I can go downstairs and ask him to come talk to me when he has calmed down. Worst case scenario, I can leave and go to my mother's house until he is ready to talk calmly."

Now that you have a plan for the worst-case scenario, think about how you would like the exchange to go. "I understand he will be upset, but I would like it if we can discuss the matter calmly." This is a tall order because you don't control him, but there are a number of things you can do to "decrease the likelihood he yells."

First, consider how you deliver the news. Maybe you can deliver the news in a text message. You can include an apology, point out that the golf club was left lying in the middle of the garage, and request that he be ready to talk calmly when he comes home. Or you can invite him into the living room, ask him to sit down, and begin by discussing how much you love him and how you feel when he yells. Then break the news. If he begins to yell, implement the plan you developed earlier: wait a few minutes, go to another room, or go to your mother's house.

In the model

As in chapter 4 with *should* statements, we are working in the bubble of perceptions. There is a slight twist here, however. Up to this point, we have been talking about how we perceive or distort the reality of what occurred or is occurring. However, this chapter discussed how when we worry, we are actually choosing to ignore reality altogether and instead focus on our imagination. Thus, our primary emotion that we experience is truly self-inflicted.

ANER MANAGEMENT:

Chapter 5 Study Questions

Take a worry and work through the template below so that you are addressing a potential issue realistically, reasonably, and effectively.

1. I am concerned that…
   _____
   _____

2. What would I do if that actually happens or turns out to be true?

   a. _____
   b. _____
   c. _____

3. What would I like to see occur?
   _____
   _____

4. What can I do to increase the likelihood that my desired future occurs?

   a. _____
   b. _____
   c. _____

5. Do it.

CHAPTER 6

EMOTIONAL WELL-BEING

Stress

Have you ever noticed that stress and anger seem to go hand in hand? In fact, isn't that often what you blame for your outbursts? "I'm sorry about what I said to you last night. Please forgive me. It is just that I have been under a lot of stress lately."

Some people enjoy stress. They say they thrive on it. So why should you be concerned about stress? Beyond the fact that for most people, it can be uncomfortable or you are more susceptible to snapping at others, it is bad for your health. In a brilliant study by Kroenke and Mangelsdorf published in the *American Journal of Medicine* in 1989, the authors researched one thousand visits to a family practice and found that 74 percent of all medical complaints were caused by stress (figure G).

ANGER MANAGEMENT:

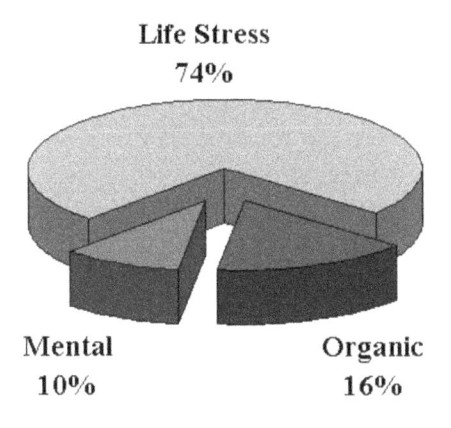

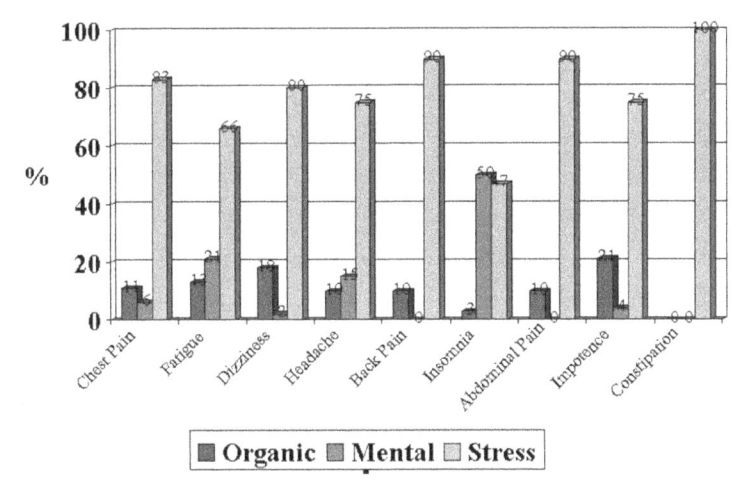

Life Stress
74%

Mental
10%

Organic
16%

■ Organic ■ Mental □ Stress

Figure G. Top Medical Complaints By Etiology

Notice in figure G that the authors were able to categorize the patient complaints into three broad categories—those complaints with an organic source (what we think of as medical issues), complaints with a mental health source, and complaints that were from the stress of life. What is more interesting is that the authors also found that when the patients' problems were treated cross category (i.e., stress problem treated organically or organic problem treated as a mental illness), the problem worsened.

Are you one of those people who pop ibuprofen every day, have one or two bottles of pink stuff in your refrigerator? This may be why you keep returning to the doctor for years with the same complaint. Your problem may not be *medical*. Perhaps you are experiencing physical *symptoms* of stress.

As a psychologist, I once treated a gentleman who was experiencing severe depression, suicidal thoughts, and voices. Certainly, there were mental-health issues needing addressed, but once he switched jobs from a high-pressure, commission-based sales position that involved a great deal of travel to a lower-stress job as a product representative with a regular schedule and a stable salary, his depression lifted, thoughts of suicide abated, and the voices ceased.

Another example of stress being related to medical issues cropped up with a client who worked for a very unpleasant and demanding boss. For years, they underwent medical treatment for irritable bowel syndrome (IBS), but once they left that job, they no longer suffered from IBS.

So learning to manage your stress can be extremely helpful for your health. But now let's look at how managing your stress can help you manage your anger more effectively. Let's begin by looking at how the brain processes basic data.

Autonomic nervous system

If we could slow time down—I mean really, really slow—this is what you would see happening. First, a beam of light leaves the sun and travels across the sky, striking an object. That beam of light is reflected toward you. At that point in time, as far as your brain knows, nothing exists. This is because the beam of light has not yet made it to your eye. The beam of light would continue to travel and eventually strike the back of your eye. There, it stimulates a nerve that, in turn, sends a signal (data) down the optic nerve into the brain.

At this point in time, still nothing exists. We simply have data leaving the eyeball and traveling through the brain. This data eventually reaches the occipital lobe, where the data is organized—critical shapes, features, textures etc.—but still no object exists because all your brain has done at this point is organize the visual data.

After the data is organized, it is reviewed by another region of the brain where the object is now identified. "Aardvark. No, dog. No. I know. It is a bear!" This is a decision. Your brain decided it is a *bear* and not a *dog*.

But the object has only been identified. The next step is to decide how you feel about *bears*. Your brain begins evaluating the *bear* and the context in which you are seeing it. Your brain might say, "Hmm, what do I know about bears? They are large, dangerous, and this one is staring right at me. I am alone in the woods, and my car is not nearby. This is a threat!" This, too, is a decision. If instead of being alone in the woods, you were standing in the zoo, you would decide this bear is not a threat.

Once you decide that the bear is a threat, a signal is sent to an old part of the brain called the autonomic nervous system. This portion of the brain is responsible for regulating all your bodily functions. You do not control this portion of the brain. Don't believe me? Make yourself start sweating. How about shifting your heart rate to forty beats per minute, then up to seventy-two beats. See what I mean? You don't control this part of your brain, but this part of your brain controls your body. When you determine that you are being threatened, this region of the brain prepares the body to deal with the threat.

In addition to physical preparedness, you are also made mentally prepared. You're walking through the woods, enjoying the day, thinking about many different things, then suddenly, the bear appears. Your body is energized and prepared to face the threat, and your mind is suddenly focused on nothing but the bear—tunnel vision. In this moment, you are only capable of three basic thoughts: Threat, Fight or Flight.

In order to survive this encounter, your attention is sharply focused on the threat and a couple of basic options to ensure your survival. In this moment, you no longer notice the beautiful trees, the cool breeze, the thoughts of retirement, or the grocery list. Your brain will not let you think of those things. If you are going to survive, you must have all your mental capacity focused on the threat in front of you and immediate options to respond either by fighting the bear or running in the other direction.

"How does all this relate to stress?" you ask. Simple. This is stress. It is also anxiety. It is also anger. Read back through the explanation. Notice that the *bear* did not activate the autonomic nervous system. It was *your decision* that the bear posed a *threat* that activated the system. Decisions are thoughts. Since thoughts can activate the autonomic nervous system, you don't actually need the bear present. You just need the *thought* that *you* are being threatened.

When the threat is standing in front of you, we tend to call it fear. When the threat is in your imagination (worries, for example), we call it anxiety. When the threat is real but not present (deadlines at work, traffic, bills, etc.), we call it stress. Sometimes we choose to respond to the threat with *fight* instead of flight. In those instances, we may call it anger. But the common denominator, no matter what we call it, is the activation of the autonomic nervous system.

Hopefully, you are beginning to see how these things work together. As you become fearful or worried or stressed, your body becomes energized, and your mental focus narrows to just the threat. This narrowing of attention may be good when dealing with a bear in the woods, but it creates a lot of problems in the rest of your life.

As your thoughts narrow down on the threat, you begin to see fewer and fewer options for handling the situation. Have you ever reacted to someone or something when under stress and later, maybe the next day, regretted it? Maybe you said, "Geez! I made such a big deal out of that. If I would've only done this instead of that, the problem would have been solved!" Because of that narrowing of focus, you are incapable of seeing other options and more likely to react by leaving, escaping, running away, denial, or by lashing out at the threat.

How do you know when you are stressed out, anxious, irritable, frustrated? We all experience stress differently. That is due to how our body expresses it. Maybe one person's muscles tense a little more than normal, so they have a lot of tension headaches. For another person, their heart rate and blood pressure may go higher, so they tend to get dizzy when under stress. It is important to know your signs of stress because the sooner you recognize it happening, the sooner you can begin turning the stress off so that you can think more clearly and effectively in the situation. Review the signs and symptoms of stress in the following figure.

Common Signs of Stress

Frequent headaches
Jaw clenching or gritting and grinding of teeth
Stuttering or stammering
Tremors, trembling of lips or hands
Neck ache, back pain, muscle spasms
Lightheadedness, faintness, dizziness
Frequent blushing, sweating
Cold or sweaty hands or feet
Dry mouth, problems swallowing
Frequent colds, infections, herpes sores
Rashes, itching, hives, goose bumps
Increased or decreased appetite
Heartburn, stomach pain, nausea
Excess belching, flatulence
Constipation, diarrhea
Difficulty breathing, sighing
Sudden attacks of panic
Chest pain, palpitations, frequent urination
Excess worry, guilt, nervousness
Increased anger, frustration, hostility
Insomnia, nightmares, disturbing dreams
Difficulty concentrating, racing thoughts
Trouble learning new information
Forgetfulness, disorganization, confusion
Difficulty in making decisions
Feeling overloaded or overwhelmed
Crying spells
Little interest in appearance, punctuality

Nervous habits, fidgeting, feet tapping
Overreaction to petty annoyances
Excessive defensiveness or suspiciousness
Social withdrawal and isolation
Constant tiredness, weakness, fatigue
Frequent use of over-the-counter drugs
Weight gain or loss without diet
Increased smoking, alcohol, or drug use
Excessive gambling or impulse buying

Figure G

How to turn the autonomic nervous system off

Now that you understand how the autonomic nervous system is activated when we feel fear, stress, anxiety, or anger, understanding how to turn it off is easy. Simply take control of the things you control.

You don't control the heart rate, blood pressure, adrenal glands, but you do control the breathing. Remember, when the autonomic nervous system activates, it causes you to fill the lungs and hold it up in your chest. Since you have decided you want to feel relaxed, start by controlling your breathing. If your body responds to stress, fear, anxiety, and anger by upper-chest breathing, then you simply choose to breathe in the opposite fashion—diaphragmatic breathing.

Below your lungs is a muscle called the diaphragm. By drawing it downward, you pull your lungs downward, and they inflate into your belly. This is also known as yoga breathing or belly breathing. You intentionally choose to draw your breath into your belly, so it swells up like a balloon. The second step is to hold it for one second. This is key because this is the action that communicates to the brain, "Hey, I am in control, and I want to feel more relaxed." The final step is to simply let the breath go. After you take a belly breath, simply breathe normally for a bit then take another belly breath.

So now that you have taken charge of your body, begin to take control of your mind. Have a brief conversation with yourself. It should go something like this:

"Okay, I'm feeling stressed out right now, and when I am like this, I can't think very well, so I want to feel more relaxed so I feel better and can think more clearly. For the next few minutes, I am going to set all my problems aside. I can pick them back up in a second. They are not going anywhere. But for the next few minutes, I am going to choose to concentrate on the sounds that I am hearing. When a sound captures my attention, I will try and visualize the thing making that sound."

Once you set the agenda for yourself for the next few minutes, take a belly breath and let it go. Concentrate on the sounds. Visualize the scene where the sound is coming from. Maybe you hear a car out on the street. See the car. See the street. Picture it in your mind. Every couple of minutes, intentionally take a belly breath. While you are listening, visualizing, and breathing, occasionally tell yourself this: "Yesterday is gone. Tomorrow is a million miles away. Right here, right now, this is the moment I control. If I want to feel more relaxed, I simply choose to take a belly breath and concentrate on something that is not exciting or worrisome. When I feel calmer, I can open my eyes."

So in short, first, control the body; second, control the mind; and third, control the situation. Once you feel calmer, more relaxed, more serene, you will be able to think clearer. Adopt more realistic perspectives. And when you begin to address the problem, you will be able to generate more effective options than simply fight or flight.

Program for managing your stress

Decrease the number of stressors. Eliminate as many stressors as you can. Don't take on new ones that you can avoid. Learn to say *no*. Reduce the amount of involvement in some of the stressors. Prioritize the remaining stressors. Work on the As first; do the Cs last or not at all.

Think about your stressors differently. Identify Cognitive Distortions such as Black-White thinking, Overgeneralizing, Fortune-Telling, or Should statements. Replace them with more accurate perceptions. Find something positive, some meaning or opportunity to be derived from the stress or crisis. Focus on what you control in the situation rather than what you don't control.

Prepare yourself to deal with the stress. Adopt a healthy lifestyle—good nutrition, exercise, sleep, and play. Avoid alcohol, drugs, and nicotine. Increase your spirituality. Learn Assertiveness Skills. Learn Time Management.

Guilt

It is very important to understand guilt and shame, as it is a primary emotion that is often misunderstood and avoided at all costs. Many times, when we feel guilty, we become defensive or blaming. We do not like to be reminded of the bad things we did, so we defend ourselves from our own judgment by minimizing what we did or arguing with the person who mentioned it. We need them to stop mentioning it so we don't have to think about it and feel the pain of our guilt. We have worked hard to make it seem okay and to avoid remembering it. We may have even tried to make up for our mistake through some compensatory action. We said were sorry. We bought flowers. We bought them lots of Christmas presents. We acted good for two whole weeks. And then they mention it again, and *boom!* We go off. "Why do you have to keep bringing up the past?" "It's been two weeks! Let it go!"

Or maybe we are so unable to handle our guilt, so we blame others to justify our actions. We rationalize away our bad behavior by saying things like, "I wouldn't have drunk so much if my boss hadn't been so hard on me." "I told her she was pushing me too much and what would happen if she kept it up." "If he didn't want to get bit, he shouldn't have tried to run with the big dogs!" By making it seem as if our behavior was a simple, natural response to others around us, we do not have to take any responsibility for our actions. Therefore, we have nothing to feel guilty about.

The problem is we are twisting reality. We are minimizing our actions and their impact on others. We are shifting responsibility away from where it truly lies (in us), and we are threatening other people to keep quiet, lest we remember what we did and feel those uncomfortable feelings again.

But God gave us the ability to feel guilt for a reason, so there must be some way to use it for good. Guilt is an emotion designed to highlight our behaviors that create pain for others. It is urging us to take specific actions so that we do not perform this behavior again and hopefully bring healing to the relationship.

A client once said she has felt guilty for eleven years because her son is in foster care. She said she has tried to let it go, just accept she made a mistake, and "not dwell on it." I told her this is the wrong approach, and I want her to dwell on it. The client was flabbergasted.

This opened the door for a discussion on what emotions are and what they can do for us. We discussed guilt and how guilt is telling her that she has done something that has hurt someone else. The emotion is urging her to focus on her behaviors and analyze what she did that led to the offensive behavior. The guilt wants her to apologize and acknowledge her offensiveness and also develop a plan to correct her behavior or what led to the behavior and then implement the plan so that she reduces the likelihood of reoffending.

Only by allowing herself to feel guilty can she do this and become a better person. If she pushes the guilt aside and writes it off as a mistake, then she has no motivation, no urging to evaluate herself and make improvements. She robs herself of the determination to set a new course in life and carry through.

Steps to harness the power of guilt

1. Focus on what you did wrong and how it hurt someone else.
2. Analyze what led you to performing the offensive behavior.
3. Develop a plan to change *what led you* to performing the offensive behavior.
4. Go to the injured party and apologize for the specific thing you did wrong and how you injured them specifically.

5. Share with the other party what led to your actions (not excuse your actions) and what your plan is now to decrease the likelihood that you do it again.
6. Now go and implement your plan.

Sometimes a simple illustration helps to understand the six-step model above. Imagine you have an appointment with me at 11:00 a.m. You arrive on time and take a seat in my lobby. Then 11:00 a.m. comes and goes. Now it is 11:15 a.m., and I am nowhere to be seen. How are you feeling? You ask staff if your appointment will begin soon, and they simply say, "Please have a seat. The doctor will be with you shortly." So you sit.

At 11:30 a.m., I enter the front door with my jacket on, wearing a backpack, and I remove my sunglasses. I say to you simply, "Hello. Come with me to my office." What would you be feeling? What would you be thinking?

Now imagine instead, I walk in and say, "Hey, sorry about that. Come on in." Does my simple apology make you feel better? I said I'm sorry.

Now imagine, I walk in and say, "Hey, sorry. Traffic was really bad. Come on in." Does my apology coupled with an excuse make you feel better?

But what if I came in and said, "Listen. I am so sorry for making you sit here waiting for me and wasting your time. I did not allow enough time for travel from the clinic to the office. I thought I could make it more quickly than I did. What I have decided to do is tell my staff to allow at least thirty minutes for me to travel between offices. That way, I will be on time next week, and you will not have to wait" (these are steps 1 through 5 of the above model)? I bet before I finish the sentence, you are probably saying, "Don't worry about it. It happens."

Next week, when you arrive and I am in my office ready to go (I followed through and did step 6), could you imagine yourself grinning and saying, "Hey, doc, how was traffic today?"

Now think about it. The thing I did wrong became the thing that drew us closer together. By letting myself feel guilty, I handled the matter in such a way that allowed me to make corrections to my behavior and, in doing so, demonstrate to you that I respect and value you. My deeds match my words. You begin to feel closer to me. If I shut down my guilt, I have no motivation to make any changes, and I miss an opportunity to strengthen our relationship.

Forgiveness

You may have noticed in the preceding example of how to handle guilt, it ended with you forgiving me (tacitly or implicitly). You can't make others forgive you, but in order to make it easier for them to find forgiveness for you, it is important to handle your guilt as outlined above. However, not everyone will.

Since we can't control others, it is important for us to learn how to forgive even when they do not seek it from us and especially when they don't deserve it. You see, forgiveness is for the forgiver, not the forgiven. Forgiveness is the mental and/or spiritual process of ceasing to feel resentment, indignation, or anger against another person or ceasing to demand punishment or restitution.

When I forgive someone, I am not giving them a free pass. My forgiveness is not an endorsement of what they did. Instead, I am choosing how I am going to feel. I am choosing how I will live my life. I control me—my behavior, my thoughts, and my feelings—nothing else. So the question is, how do I want to feel? Not, have they earned my forgiveness? They never can. They can never make it up to you. Remember from the chapter on Boundaries? They don't have the ability to control you or how you feel, so there is nothing they can do that will cause you to cease feeling anger or resentment. That is solely up to you.

Even if you don't feel they deserve your forgiveness or have done anything to earn it, forgiving them sets you free from them. I once heard a parable about two monks. It was a day of fasting, so they could not talk or interact with others. They had to spend the day in prayer. However, these two particular monks had to travel to another monastery.

As they walked through the forest, they came upon a treacherous river. There was a young lady holding a baby and looking rather scared and helpless. The first monk approached her and said, "What is wrong, my dear?"

She replied, "My baby is sick, and I must get him to the village to see the doctor, but I am unable to cross this river."

So the first monk picked up the baby and carried her across the river and set the baby down. He returned and carried the young mother across the river and set her down. She scooped up her baby, thanked the monk, and hurried off to the village.

The second monk joined the first monk, and they continued their journey in silence. They arrived at the other monastery, and when the sun set and they could break fast, the second monk came and found the first monk. He said, "I am so angry with you, brother!"

The first monk asked, "Why?"

The second monk replied, "You broke your vows! You spoke to that woman! You even carried her across the river!"

The first monk replied, "Yes, but I set her down. You have been carrying her all day."

Do you see? The first monk was not *causing* the second monk's anger and resentment. The second monk chose to carry the anger and resentment all day. He was feeding it while he walked in silence. He was going over and over what the first monk had done wrong. He planned his confrontation. The second monk's journey was miserable, and he blamed the first monk for his misery. Had the second monk chosen to forgive the first monk, he could have set his anger down at the river's edge, where the first monk set the lady down, and then he would have been able to return his focus to his prayers and had a more peaceful journey.

Forgiveness is a process. I suggest the steps below. It may take time, and the steps may need to be retraced more than once.

Steps to forgiveness

1. Identify specifically what they did that you are harboring resentment for. Be specific. What did they do? How did

it affect you? What are the lasting results? Exactly what are they responsible for? Why might they have done it? (Evaluate any should statements.)
2. Identify your responsibilities in the situation. Again, be specific.
3. Affirmatively forgive them. "I am forgiving them for their actions that brought these results into my life. They made their choice for their reasons, which I do not control."
4. Now shift your attention to what you could have done to avoid the offence and to what you can do now to take care of yourself in the present and in the future.
5. If there is compensation that needs to be repaid, seek it out in a matter-of-fact, purpose-driven, and legal fashion.
6. If there are conditions to future relationships, make them known and give them the responsibility and choice to restore the relationship.
7. Recite the Serenity Prayer, "God grant me the serenity to accept the things I cannot change, the courage to change the things I can, and the wisdom to know the difference," or a prayer of your choosing.
8. Repeat steps 3 through 7 often.

Chapter 6 Study Questions

1. Practice makes perfect. Each time you practice the belly-breathing relaxation exercise, you grow in your ability to relax more deeply and more quickly each time. Set a schedule to practice relaxation each day. I recommend you do it for five minutes right after lunch before you go back to work and when you lay down to go to sleep at night.

    Monday   _____
    Tuesday   _____
    Wednesday   _____
    Thursday   _____
    Friday   _____
    Saturday   _____
    Sunday   _____

2. Using the guide in this chapter, write up your plan to adopt a healthy lifestyle (use additional paper if necessary).

3. Using the steps to deal with Guilt provided in this chapter on page 67, work through one situation in which you have experienced feelings of guilt. Sit down with someone you trust and talk through your work. Consider the benefit of putting your plan into action.

4. Using the steps to deal with Forgiveness provided in this chapter on page 70, forgive someone you have been harboring resentment toward. Sit down with someone you trust and talk through your work. Consider the benefit of putting your plan into action.

Chapter 7

Assertiveness

Let's face it. Why are you reading this book? You have a problem with someone else. Maybe more than one person. Maybe you have problems with your spouse, your coworker, your boss, your family, your neighbor, and your children. One gentleman I worked with agreed to be interviewed by a local television station doing a series on health-related issues. The television anchor asked him, "Did you know you had a problem with anger?"

He replied honestly and with great insight, "No, I didn't have a problem. Everyone else had a problem."

Hopefully, by this point in the book, you are beginning to realize that other people are not the problem, and you are not the problem. The problem is created when you don't use your anger in the way it was designed to be used. The problem is that you don't know how to interact with other people in a way that moves you toward problem resolution. You argue. You fight. You blame. You demand apologies. You offend others by the tone of your voice. You have the belief that they must change, take it back, and make it up to you. They have to change, not you.

Arguing is about winning. Where there is a winner, there is a loser. This is not problem resolution; this is dominance. Assertiveness is about solutions.

Let me give you an example of assertiveness. Think about grocery shopping. There you are, walking down the grocery aisle, pushing your cart. You are looking for Rotel Tomatoes. You move slowly, scanning the shelf to your right. Silently, you think, *Where are the tomatoes? And what is a Rotel?*

Then something catches your attention. Up ahead, another shopper turns into the aisle you're shopping in and slowly heads toward you. They are preoccupied looking for some other product. Pushing their cart, they slowly move in your direction. But since they are about forty to fifty feet away, you don't do anything.

You return to your shopping. "Tomatoes, tomatoes, tomatoes." But now, every few seconds, you cast a quick glance up ahead to see where the other shopper is. Shop, shop, glance. Shop, shop, glance. Shop, glance, shop. You continue to do nothing special. Just walk slowly and continue to shop. But at some point, they draw near enough, and you finally act (I bet you $100 you do the following). You veer your shopping cart to the right, catch their eye, politely nod, and cast a quick smile. You then return to your shopping.

Now stop and think about this for a minute. Why do you move your cart to the right? Because you are a nice person. You are polite. You are courteous. You have no desire to offend the other shopper. In other words, you want to share this shopping experience with them.

Now what *allows* you to do this? It is your ability to predict where they begin and end in time and space. In space, you can see their physicality. You can see where their body begins and ends. In time, you can determine their trajectory based on their present location, rate of movement, layout of the grocery aisle. You are able to predict when they will be close to you. Your ability to predict where the other shopper is in time and space informs you when you are approaching their physical *boundaries*. Having this knowledge, you are empowered to choose, at the proper moment, to respect their physical *boundaries* and move your shopping cart.

Now it is clear you are able to understand where a person begins and ends physically, but where do they begin and end personally? What are their personal *boundaries*? What makes that person happy? Sad? What would irritate them? You don't know. You are able to see another person's physical boundaries but not their personal boundaries. Think about this next question for a minute before reading ahead to the answer. If the relationship in question is going to work out, who is responsible for learning all they can about the other person?

This is a tough question for some people. There tends to be a knee-jerk response. "Well, it is my responsibility to find out, so I do not offend them." But that is not the correct answer. A personal boundary is an intellectual concept. What one finds offensive, another may find humorous. We can't know everything about everybody, and it would be ridiculous to expect that we would interview every single person we came in contact with to develop a full understanding of their personal boundaries before interacting with them.

The correct answer is it is our *own* responsibility to learn about ourselves. What makes me happy or sad? What are my politics, my sense of humor? You can't read another person's mind, but you can learn your own. Now for the relationship to work, since they can't read your mind either, it is your responsibility to inform others of your personal boundaries.

Certainly, we have rules of thumb to follow:

Never discuss politics and religion.

Watch your language in mixed company.

But if someone begins to tell a joke about three nuns who go into a bar, and you do not like religious humor, are they at fault for offending you? How were they to know this about you? So if this relationship is going to be successful, you have to be able to tell them something about yourself. This is called assertiveness.

Assertiveness is not confrontation. Confrontation is confrontation. Assertiveness is simply letting others know something about you they may not have known. So if someone begins telling the joke about three nuns, you might assert yourself by raising your hand and saying, "I'm sorry, you may not have known this, but I am not into religious humor." You just asserted yourself. You put something of yourself out there for others to see. Now it is up to them to decide how to respond.

If you were the one telling the joke, and I said to you, "I am not comfortable with religious humor," I just shared with you my personal boundary. You can now see where I begin and end personally. How might you respond? Are you going to "move your shopping cart" and share this experience with me, or are you going to barge right ahead and run over my boundary?

The vast majority of us will choose to move our shopping cart. Most of us don't want to offend others, and our reaction to being told by someone that they do not like that type of humor would be much like our reaction if we looked up as we almost accidentally bumped into someone's shopping cart in the grocery story. We would physically freeze or jump back. We might hold up our hands and quickly say, "Oh, I'm sorry!" And this is what many people do in response to being shown a personal boundary. When told, "hey, I don't like religious humor," the jokester very often holds his hands up, leans back, and says something to the effect, "Sorry! Didn't mean to offend!"

Through the use of assertiveness, you can take your problem to another person in an attempt to elicit their help in solving the matter. Confrontation is not necessary.

Being assertive

Being assertive is simple. The basic formula is, "I feel _____ when you _____." Remember, you are asserting *yourself,* not confronting their behavior. Talk about *you*, not them. If you have to mention them, be factual. Don't label or judge their behavior but state their behavior. If you label their behavior, we will spend all day arguing about the label. But if you state the behavior, there is nothing to argue about.

Confrontational sentence: "Hey, I sat around all day yesterday waiting on you, and you blew me off!" In this sentence, we don't really know anything about the speaker. They sat around all day, but is that good or bad? They also waited. Is waiting the problem, or is sitting around the problem? And how was this a problem? Are they feeling mad, sad, hurt, rejected, taken for granted? Further, we don't actually know what the other person did that was wrong. The speaker says, "You blew me off!" Do we know this for a fact? Might they have had an emergency that took precedent?

Assertive sentence: "Hey, you told me you would come by and pick up that box yesterday. I made sure I was home so you could. I'm a little upset because I turned down an invitation to a movie so I could be there to let you in, but you never showed." This sentence is a lot clearer. You know exactly what the behavior of the other person was that is problematic and how the speaker felt. The speaker asserted specific facts to reduce the chance of arguing and to keep the conversation focused on the topic.

Distracting responses

Now being assertive is easy. *Remaining* assertive—that is the hard part. You know what I am talking about. How many times have you stewed or worried over a matter? You talked to friends, you prayed on the matter, and when you finally worked up the courage to say something to the other person, somehow or another, the conversation didn't go the way you expected it to, and you ended up defending yourself or, worse, apologizing. How did that happen?

You were distracted. You made your big assertive statement, and they did something that got you completely off topic. These are called Distracting Responses, and they are sometimes called Blocking Gambits because people may respond to you in such a manner as to block you from discussing or getting what you want. Study these and prepare for them. As you read them, notice the explanation of each refers to specific Assertiveness Techniques you can use to counter the Blocking Gambit. Those techniques are found immediately following the list of Distracting Responses.

Accusing Gambit, The other person blames you for the problem you have identified. ("You are always so slow cooking dinner that I am too tired to clean the kitchen by the time we get to eat.") Counter with the Clouding technique. ("That may be so, but you're still breaking your agreement to do the dishes.") Or simply disagree, pointing out the error in their contention. ("I do not believe that 8:00 p.m. is too late to do the dishes.")

The Beat-Up. This happens when you make an assertion, and the other person responds by making a personal attack. ("Who are you to be talking about monopolizing the conversation? You're the biggest loudmouth around!") Counter with Assertive Irony ("Thank you very much!") or Broken Record ("You may think so, but I have observed that…") or Defusing ("I can see your angry right now. Let's talk about this after the meeting").

Delaying Gambit. The other person responds to your request with, "Not now. I'm too tired," or "I'll do it later." Use the Broken Record technique ("Eight p.m. is not too late to do the dishes").

Denial. The other person says, "I did not do that," or "You misunderstood me." Assert what you observed and experienced using Clouding ("It may seem that way to you, but I have noticed that…").

Laughing It Off. This is an extremely common technique. People respond to your assertion as if it were a joke. ("Your kidding! I am only three weeks late? Ha!") Use the Content-to-Process Shift ("Humor is getting us off track here" or "I have noticed that each time I bring up how you don't follow through, you make a joke about it") or the Broken Record ("Yes, but…").

Quibbling. The other person doesn't outright deny your assertion, but they quibble about the legitimacy of what you're saying ("Oh, I am sure it's not that big a deal") or the magnitude of your problem. Use Clouding ("You're right. It's not the end of the world, but it has been bothering me a lot") or the Content-to-Process Shift ("We are arguing about how much of a problem it is right now. The important thing is that it is a problem to me").

Threatening. The other person threatens you. Use Defusing ("I see you're angry. Let's talk about this after dinner"), the Circuit Breaker ("This is a serious issue" or "Perhaps so"), or Assertive Inquiry ("What is it that is bothering you?").

Why Gambit. Everything you say is met with a *why* response ("Why do you think that?" or "Why don't you want to go?"). Use the Content-to-Process Shift ("Why isn't the point. The point is that I don't want to go") or the Broken Record ("I can see you're bothered by my decision, but I really don't want to go out tonight").

ANGER MANAGEMENT:

Remaining assertive

Below is a list of specific ways to counter Distracting Responses and remain assertive. Some may seem surprising. Remember, assertiveness is simply letting other people know something about you. You are asserting yourself, so even asking a question is considered assertive because you are saying, "I am lacking information" or "I am not understanding. I would like more information so I can proceed."

Assertive Agreement. Answer their criticism by acknowledging you've made an error ("You're right. I did forget our lunch date"), but separate that mistake from any suggestion you are a bad person ("I am usually more responsible").

Assertive Delay. If you find the discussion is getting heated, and someone is challenging you, rather than lose your composure, delay making a full response until you are able to formulate an appropriate reply ("Yes, you make an interesting point. I will have to give that some thought. Can we continue this conversation later?").

Assertive Irony. Simply answer positively. If someone calls you a *loudmouth*, just say, "Thank you!" and smile. Once you react positively, reassert your original request or statement. "Now that we have established that I am a loudmouth, I still want you to go and do the dishes."

Broken Record. Steer the conversation back on track by simply repeating your initial assertive statement ("Yes, I know, but the point is…" or "I agree, but as I was saying…").

Circuit Breaker. Put a lid on the flow of griping or criticism coming from someone by using single-word or extremely brief responses ("Yes…," "No…," "Perhaps…"). In doing so, you are helping them end one criticism so they can move to the next. The purpose here is to help them vent, say their piece, and get through with whatever they are saying so you can *get back to* what you originally asserted. Once they are done, try summarizing and restating your assertion. ("I understand you're very angry about having to do chores, but the fact remains it is your turn on the schedule to do dishes.") Once the dishes are done, you can always come back to their venting and anything they said and address it as a problem.

Clouding. This is a kind of verbal sleight of hand in which you appear to give ground without actually doing so. Agree with the other person's argument, but don't agree to change ("You may be right. Maybe I don't help out around the house as much as I could.") Once you cloud, then return the conversation back to the topic you asserted. Other Clouding phrases might me, ("That's interesting…," "That's possible…," "You may have a point.")

Content-to-Process Shift. You intentionally shift the focus from the actual topic for a moment to analyze what is happening between the two of you right now. You do this in order to clear up a distraction so you can get back to the topic. ("We're getting off the subject now." "We have been sidetracked into talking about other issues." "You seem to be angry with me." "Why is it whenever I bring this up, you laugh and walk away?")

Defusing. If the other becomes angry, defuse the situation by ignoring the content of their anger and put off further discussion until they have cooled down. ("I can see that you are angry right now. Let's talk about this later, perhaps this afternoon.") For the more advanced, you can do this on the fly in the middle of the conversation. You ignore their anger and speak directly to the topic. You don't react or respond to their yelling or curse words or red face. You ignore those behaviors and speak only about the topic. When you remain calm and talk sensibly, they are forced to evaluate their own actions. If they see they are being inappropriate or overreacting, they will use you as a model and begin to talk about the matter more calmly.

In the model

Assertiveness is where the rubber meets the road. This is the final product. As you begin to understand and apply all the previous chapters, they all build to this moment. Take the problem and address it with someone else. There are no shortcuts. Each step in the model is equally important, and this step is no exception. This is how you apply all that you have learned. Once you know what the problem is and you have clarified all your perceptions, once you have wrestled with the fairness of the matter and consulted with others about the situation, once you have decided that you will need to talk to the other person about the situation, you assert yourself. You explain how you are feeling, what you are wanting, and maybe what would be a good alternative. You work to keep yourself focused on the matter at hand and redirect the conversation back to the main topic when it starts to veer off course by using the Remaining Assertive techniques. These are the actions that will increase the likelihood of your success.

Chapter 7 Study Questions

1. What is assertiveness?

2. Identify a time when you were angry and assertiveness would have helped you achieve a successful outcome.

3. Write how you could respond assertively in the following situations. Use the techniques in this chapter.

    a. Someone steps in front of you while you're in line at the grocery store.

    b. Your son points out your hypocrisy for telling him not to smoke even though you smoke.

c. Your spouse continues to spend money in a way that does not fit in the budget the two of you originally agreed to establish.

4. Now go and practice these skills. If you are in a class, the instructor should set up some role plays for the students. If you're not in class or you want additional practice, set up safe scenarios. Slip it in at work. Sneak it in at home. Or be bolder. Go to the store and purchase a small item. After purchasing it, take your receipt and the item and walk over to the return counter and tell the clerk you have changed your mind about the purchase and would like to return it. Ask for a special order at the restaurant, something not on the menu. The next time you have to make a substantial purchase at one of the national chain stores, tell the clerk or manager that you would like to purchase the item, but you would really appreciate it if they could give you a 10 percent discount. Try out the assertiveness techniques, but most importantly, evaluate how other people respond to you when you are being assertive. How did they react? Was it negative or positive? Do your interactions go differently when you use these techniques?

CHAPTER 8

LISTENING

This will be a fairly short chapter. It is not complicated. Simply shut up. So many of our problems in relationships can be solved by simply listening to what the other person has to say.

Pay attention to this true story. I was assigned a case by the Court and asked to mediate a dispute between two parents. My office contacted the couple and mailed them the prerequisite paperwork and contract for my fees. Both parties dutifully completed all the paperwork, set up their initial appointments, paid their fees, and took off work to come in and see me.

They were divorced and shared a daughter. She had been having problems with her grades in school. The father came in first. He explained the fifteen-year history with the mother since the divorce and how she has treated him so poorly over time. He detailed each and every transgression. He provided documents to support his position that this woman has done nothing but create problems for him over the years. She did not teach their daughter good values in her home, and this was the core of the problem. And he had a solution. Suffice to say the solution was XYZ. He then decried her unreasonableness and how she refuses to see what is right, and she has refused to adopt the plan XYZ.

I then met with the mother. She was equally angry with the father. She, too, felt compelled to lay out the fifteen-year history of their postdivorce relationship and how she has been forced to take him to Court to do what is right. She recounted the times he unfairly dragged her to Court for silly matters. She, too, had an opinion about the father's household and believed that he was teaching her daughter poor values, and to her, this was the core of the problem, and she had a solution as well. Suffice it to say the solution, from her perspective, was XYZ.

I sat there a bit stunned. I reviewed her plan with her again—XYZ. I turned in my notes to what the father had proposed—XYZ. The two of them had been in and out of Court for years. With regard to their daughter's grades, they had been fighting for the past three months over the matter. They both hired attorneys. They filed motions. They went to Court. And now they were both proclaiming they wanted the *exact same* solution—XYZ.

Surely, it was not this simple. I must be missing something. I decided to bring the two of them in for a joint meeting. On the day of the meeting, they both arrived on time but refused to wait in the same waiting room. They had to be escorted to my office to avoid conflict in the hallway.

They were seated on the same couch side by side (I did this on purpose). I had my notes fully prepared and laid out neatly in front of me. I began to explain my understanding of the problem that brought them back to Court and, eventually, to me.

As I detailed the issue surrounding the grades, they began to accuse the other of being at fault for various things. It quickly turned into a shouting match, and I just sat there in amazement. Finally, I raised my hand and waited patiently. Once they stopped yelling at each other and turned their attention to me, I said, "I have had the opportunity to speak with both of you privately. I think what would be best at this point is for me to begin this session by reading to both of you each other's proposed solution."

This seemed to satisfy both of them. They each crossed their arms and settled back on the couch with a smug look on their faces that seemed to say, "Finally! I am finally going to get my way!"

I made a bit of a production of sorting my notes and setting out the father's interview notes and the mother's interview notes side by side. I studied them both briefly and then said, "Okay, the first proposal I want to review is as follows" (I intentionally did not say whose proposal it was). I then read out loud in a very important-sounding voice, "X…Y…Z."

When I was done reading, I shuffled the papers a bit and cleared my throat and waited. After a long-enough pause that I felt each of them were equally uncomfortable, I looked up and said, "What? Were you waiting for me to read the other proposal?"

They both looked at me, and their expression said, "Yeah, I want to hear what the chump had to say."

I then dropped the hammer. "You both told me you wanted the *exact* same thing!" They shot looks of disbelief at each other and then at me. I held up both stacks of paper and repeated myself. "You both told me, when I asked you, that the best solution for this matter would be…X…Y…Z."

They were stunned. They had argued with each other for so long on so many things, they no longer could even *listen to each other for one second*. They automatically assumed the other person was wrong and didn't know anything. Even when they were saying the exact same thing, they could not hear each other.

All too often, we don't listen, and that creates many of our problems. I want to stress two components to listening in this chapter. Intentional Listening and Active listening.

Intentional listening

Too often, we bring to the table preconceived notions, assumptions, and expectations. We already know what they are going to say, and we have prepared our response. Or the moment they say something, we assume to know why they are saying it. And finally, if they don't say what we expect them to say, then this conversation is over.

Imagine for a moment any problem you have with another person. Maybe you and your spouse disagree about how to discipline the children, or you have been butting heads with your boss about how to handle a certain project. Now answer this question. Where does that problem exist? Where is the problem *located*? It is a tough question because most of the time, we say that they are the problem and don't view the problem as being separate from them or us.

The problem exists between the two of you. It is not you; it is not them. It is between the two of you. Your boss feels he must run the company a certain way in order to get the results he expects. You believe if he ran it a different way, he would get better productivity and increase morale. Where is the problem? It exists in your mind and possibly theirs. But you only see one side of the matter. Imagine holding a sheet of paper up in the air. On the side facing you, you record all your thoughts about a matter, history related to the subject, dreams, fears, and solutions. You can see all of that, but what is missing? The other side of the paper. The other party involved in this conflict is looking at the situation from their side of the paper. And on their side, you cannot see all of their thoughts about the matter, their history related to this subject, dreams, fears, and solutions.

How do you expect to solve a problem if you are only aware of half of the information? And as you saw with the couple in my office, once they were exposed to the other person's side of the paper, they found out that a problem did not actually exist. In order to solve a problem, you have to understand both sides of it. In order to understand their view of the matter, you have to listen. It is so easy for us to jump to conclusions and make assumptions or put our demands above all else. It takes an intentional effort to set ourselves aside for a time so that we can genuinely hear the other person.

So whenever you are having a problem with someone else, try to help them explain to you what is going on for them. Ask them how they are feeling, how they see the problem, what their solutions might be. You will be surprised at how far simply *listening* to another person goes toward diffusing conflicts and creating solutions.

Active listening

Active listening skills are those behaviors you perform that demonstrate to the other person that you are listening to them. Imagine what you would think if you walked into your boss' office and began telling him about a matter of urgency. While you spoke, your boss continued to look at the calendar and perform various tasks on the computer. What would you think? How would you feel?

I have met many people who do these various things, and they tell me, "But I can still hear everything they are saying." This may be true, but they are not *listening*. Listening is more than simply being able to repeat back a series of words uttered by another. It is about understanding, even connecting. When you are not looking at the speaker, engaging in other activities, and acknowledging the speaker, you leave it completely up to them to label your behavior. "They don't even care enough to stop what they are doing for five minutes! He answered the phone while I was talking to him! He must really feel I am unimportant."

People are going to read and interpret how you listen to them whether you like it or not, so focus on what you control and perform the behaviors that will send the message you are wanting them to receive: "You are important to me, and I want to hear your perspective so we can solve this matter."

Turn off the television. Turn off the TV or the video game or the radio, or put down your phone. If you are engaged in an activity when someone begins to speak to you, show them through your actions that you are choosing to make them the most important thing in your life at that very moment. By choosing them over a TV show, you are demonstrating where your priorities lie. And the same goes for interruptions. Don't let there be any. You and your spouse are discussing a matter, and the phone rings. Don't answer it. Let it go to voicemail. Better yet, say, "Excuse me. Let me put this on silent." That is why you have a voicemail feature and a volume control on the phone. With today's cellular-phone technology, you can tell who is calling. Let them wait. Make the caller the second-most-important person in this moment, not the person standing in front of you.

Body posture. Assume an open body posture. Turn your body toward them. Make eye contact. Lower your arms or extend a hand toward them with the palm up. This communicates to the other party that you are comfortable hearing from them and are open to anything they have to say. Crossing your arms, turning your body away, and looking away send the signal that you do not want to hear from them.

Encourage them. Don't rush them. Be patient. Use some simple responses to show them you are following what they have to say and want to hear more. Nod your head, use a facial expression that matches the emotion of the topic. If they say something funny, smile. If they say something sad, frown. If they express frustration, grimace. You are giving them nonverbal feedback that you are hearing them in that moment and understanding what they are communicating. Inject simple, encouraging comments such as, "I see" or "Go on" or "Tell me more." These comments do not interrupt their train of thought. Instead, you will communicate to the speaker that you are interested in learning more about what they are saying.

Summarize. This is important. You are listening for a purpose. That purpose is to try and understand the matter from their perspective (I did not say agree with them). When you are actively listening, do everything you can to get as much information from them so you could write a summary of their thoughts or their position or their experience. Your summary would be close enough to one they would write that they would accept it as their own. So when someone has told you something, take a few moments to repeat back to them what it is you think you heard them say. Be sure to clarify you are just trying to make sure you are understanding what they are trying to communicate, then summarize their comments and any meaning you gleaned. This gives them a chance to determine if they have expressed themselves clearly to you. They may have left something out or stressed the wrong thing. When you repeat back what they have just told you, it gives them a chance to clarify their statements. It also gives them conclusive proof you were listening.

In the model

This technique comes into play in many areas in the model, first and foremost at the perception stage. You have to really focus on what the other person is saying or doing in order to gather good data to formulate your perceptions. Then in steps 5 through 7, when you consult with other people, the better you are able to listen to the feedback and advice you receive from friends, family, and professionals. Then finally, in step 8, when you take your concerns or problems to other people and attempt to resolve conflict, the better you will listen to their feedback and responses, and the more success you will have in actually resolving conflict.

ANGER MANAGEMENT:

Chapter 8 Study Questions

1. What is intentional listening?

2. What is active listening?

3. This week, pick one person or situation and use all the intentional listening and active listening skills you can employ. Write below what that experience was like and how it was different than other times.

Chapter 9

Bringing It All Together

Now that you have a solid understanding of all the components of the Anger Model, let's look at how to use it. The first step you take does not involve the Anger Model at all. Remember, events do not occur in a vacuum. You are in the midst of life. Work, kids, marriage, family, neighbors, bills, traffic, and a million other things are going on all around you all the time, so if your goal is to one day manage your anger better, start by managing your life better. Refer to the chapter on Stress Management. Implement a few changes to your life that will begin to reduce the overall stress levels. Remember, stress, anxiety, fear, anger are all related to activation of the autonomic nervous system, so one makes you more vulnerable to the other.

Think of it in these terms. Picture a scale of 1 to 10. At the bottom of the scale, a 1 represents utter relaxation, and at the top of the scale, the 10 represents explosion. If you come home after a stressful workday and horrible traffic, your stress level may be at a level 6 or 7. That means you are only three to four points away from explosion. If you take steps to reduce your overall stress levels and learn relaxation techniques, then in the same scenario, your stress level may only be a 4 or a 5 when you return home.

By managing your overall stress level, you have given yourself a better chance to deal with issues as they crop up. Instead of being three to four points away from an explosion, you are four to five points away. That increases your chance of successfully handling the next situation you encounter and correctly using the skills in this book.

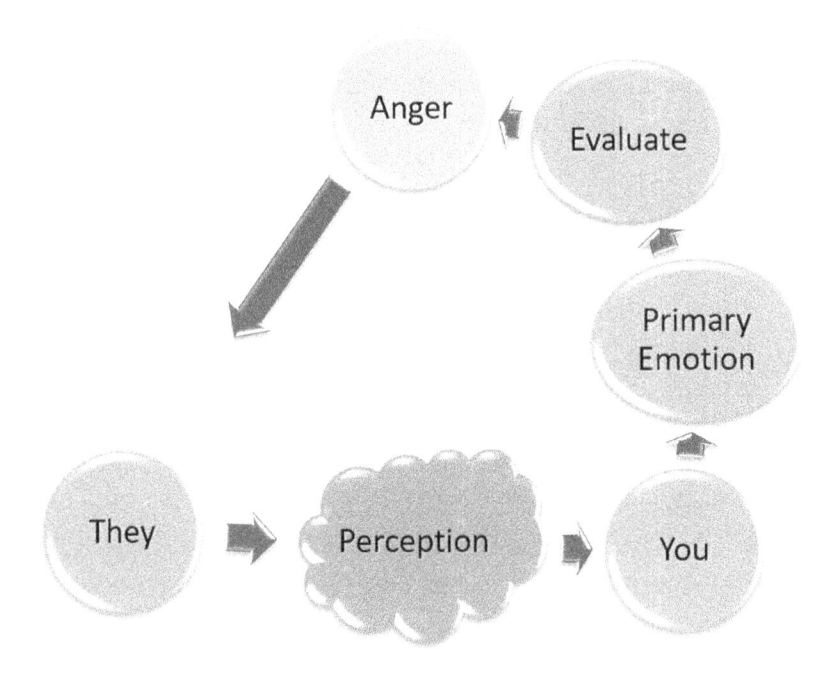

Figure B. The Anger Model

Anger Model

Over the preceding chapters, we have broken out important aspects of the Anger Model. Now you can use the model to effectively harness the power of your anger and use it to be determined, driven, and steadfast. Use your power to your *advantage*. Here is a brief summary of what we have discussed in the order you will begin to use the various skill sets.

Anger to Advantage through the Anger Model
Step-by-Step Instructions for How to Harness the Energy and Focus to Transform Anger into Advantage

1. Identify the problem. What is the negative Primary Emotion you are feeling, and how would you rather feel? (E.g., disrespected/respected, rejected/accepted, unloved/loved, threatened/safe.)
2. Analyze your perceptions. What are the facts? Are your perceptions filled with cognitive distortions such as Should Statements or Jumping to Conclusions? Reframing these thoughts may reduce the negative Primary Emotion.
3. Administer self-care. Since only you control how you feel, what can you do to decrease the negative Primary Emotion and increase the preferred emotion?
4. Consider if it must be fair. Ask yourself, "Really? Everything must be fair?"
5. Talk to friends. Get their advice, but more importantly, saying things out loud helps us hear ourselves and gain perspective.
6. Talk to clergy. Spiritual advice is valuable, and here is a second chance to talk it through out loud.
7. Talk with a professional. Some situations may require specialty advice from an attorney, real estate agent, or even a psychologist. Become knowledgeable about your situation. And again, this is a third opportunity to talk it through out loud.
8. Communicate assertively with the person you are in conflict with and truly listen to them. Approach the other person calmly, with the intention of resolving a problem or correcting a misunderstanding or improving a relationship. Present to them a summary of items 1 through 7 you just walked through, and do so in a calm, matter-of-fact manner. You can also assert to them what you would like to understand better or what you would like to see happen in the future.

ANGER MANAGEMENT:

Let's take a simple example and walk through the model. *Scenario*: Early one Tuesday afternoon, you have a great idea. Rather than the normal routine, you decide you and your wife should go to a movie that evening. You call her, and she doesn't answer. Instead, it goes to voicemail, so you leave a message in a cheery voice. "Hey, honey, give me a callback!"

Fifteen minutes pass. Then thirty minutes go by with no response, and you start to feel frustrated. After an hour and a half, you have moved beyond frustration to anger. You think, *Why is she blowing me off? I wanted to take her out tonight, but if this is how she is going to treat me, to heck with her!*

As you perform each step, monitor your *anger* and see how you feel at each stage. If you find after working one of the steps that your anger suddenly dissipates, take note of that stage because that is where you will want to concentrate additional work on yourself in the future.

1. Identify the problem. Look inside at your Primary Emotions. How are you feeling? Rejected, hurt, unloved, scared? It is important to know this because this is what you are trying to change. Then decide upon your preferred emotional state. If you are feeling rejected, you may want to feel accepted. If you are feeling scared, you may want to feel safe.
2. Analyze your perceptions
   a. First, start by detailing the *known* facts. "I called her and left a voicemail." What else? "My phone has not rung."
   b. What other thoughts were you having beyond the facts? Are you creating some of your distress through Cognitive Distortions? Look at your thoughts about the scenario. "Why is she blowing me off?" Is that a fact or a distortion? Distortion. You are Jumping to Conclusions and Reading Minds by imagining that she looked at the caller ID and hit the ignore button. Or she listened to the voicemail and then chose to

not call you back. You don't know for a fact that she is blowing you off or not. All you know is that your phone has not rung. What other reasons are there for your phone not ringing? Maybe she is in a meeting and can't call back. Maybe she didn't hear her phone, maybe she left her phone in the car, maybe her battery is dead, etc.

    c. What are underlying beliefs that you may hold that might be coloring your perceptions? "People should always return phone calls as soon as possible." This is another cognitive distortion—*should*. Is this a law? No, it is a preference. You will be better off rephrasing this belief as a preference. "I appreciate it when people return phone calls in a timely fashion."

    d. Now solidify your analysis so that your perceptions are as accurate and distortion-free as possible before moving on. "I called my wife and left a voicemail, and she has not called me back yet. I have no idea why, but I appreciate it when people return my calls as soon as possible." Now notice what is happening to your Primary Emotion. Immediately, you begin to feel less hurt and rejection.

3. Implement self-care. This is a simple example, so not much may need to be done here. Reassure yourself your wife loves you and probably has a valid reason for not calling back right away. Do some belly breathing to bring some additional calmness. Go for a walk. Work on your hobby. Call someone else to simply feel a connection.

4. Challenge the idea that life has to be fair and all things have to be right. Is this *really* an issue of fairness? Is this *really* a matter of right or wrong? You called your wife, and you're now waiting for a return call. It is not happening as fast as you would prefer. That is all.

5. Talk with friends. Talk through the situation with a trusted confidant. "Hey, Bob, I want to ask you something. I called my wife, and she hasn't called me back yet. What do you

think?" One important thing to remember about talking with family and friends: they are not trained professionals, so their advice may be biased and unhelpful. They may hold many cognitive distortions themselves, so when you talk matters out with family and friends, remember to filter what they are saying. Recognize the more important reason to talk it out with someone else is to hear yourself and to work through the scenario while considering alternative perspectives and solutions.

6. Talk with clergy. The more I practice psychology, the more I realize we have not created anything new. The Bible is full of wisdom and excellent advice. Speaking to someone knowledgeable in the Scripture can be helpful, enlightening and strengthen your walk with the Lord. Many people see religion as separate from their daily life. Hopefully, you come to realize that the Word belongs in your everyday life.

7. Talk with a professional. Maybe you're not a religious person, or the matter you're dealing with is better suited for a different type of expert. Seek out a psychologist or a family counselor or an attorney. Again, you are trying to seek out knowledge about a subject matter you may not have and giving yourself a chance to talk it through with someone else out loud.

8. Assertive conversation. Now that you have completed steps 1 through 7, you may find that the matter has been resolved, and you don't need to address it with the other person. "You know what, I called her, and she will call me back when she is able. When she does, then I will ask her to go to a movie."

Or maybe you have been following along as I walked through steps 1 through 7, and an answer became glaringly obvious. "Try calling again!" Use Assertiveness skills to seek what you want. You are excited about the date, and you are wanting to speak to her. It has been over an hour; it is okay to pick up the phone and try again.

Many times, as you begin walking through the steps, you will find that what started out as a problem ends up not being a problem at all.

Or you realize, you won't know if there is a problem or not until you finally speak to the other person. "Hey, honey, I called you earlier, and I never heard back. Is everything okay?" Now you will get your answer. Then you will have additional reality, additional facts to deal with. Maybe her phone went dead, and she was at the store all day, getting a new one, or maybe she did see you called but chose to simply wait until you came home from work to see what you called about—two different realities that will then lay out two very different pathways for you.

But if a problem truly exists that will involve the other person's cooperation to address, Assertiveness is the key to handling situations in a calm, effective, mature manner and resolving conflicts. Memorize and practice the Assertiveness Skills in chapter 7. By working your way through steps 1 through 7, you increase your self-awareness, care for yourself emotionally, and prepare yourself to discuss the matter with the other person. For that conversation to go as well as possible, you need to have solid assertiveness skills to handle the ups and downs of the discussion as it is unfolding.

When you approach the other person about the matter, use the Assertiveness Skills to assert (present) to them all that you learned when you worked through steps 1 through 7. "Hey, when you _____, I felt _____. I would appreciate it if you _____."

There is a good chance they respond positively and the two of you work out the issue, but if they respond defensively or negatively, be prepared to immediately employ the Remaining Assertive Skills to keep the conversation focused on the topic you want and moving in the direction you want. If they still refuse to cooperate, you have validated yourself and are free to further assert what you will do next. "Well, in that case, this is how I will handle things next time."

ANGER MANAGEMENT:

Chapter 9 Homework

Take the time to make copies of the Anger Management Model Template in the back of this book. Consider various scenarios you struggle with and use the template to walk through each scenario. Share your work with the class and get feedback from others. If you are reading this book on your own, work through some examples on your own, then find a friend, spouse, pastor, or therapist you can trust. Share your work with them and seek their feedback. Practice makes perfect.

As discussed at the outset of the book, most "anger problems" are the result of trying not to be angry. You bottle it up and hold it in only to eventually explode. But there are other important factors that lead to unnecessary anger, such as you are distorting the reality of the situation by creating inappropriate expectations (Shoulds) of others or yourself, or you are Jumping to Conclusions and imagining the worst. But most often, it is a combination of all these elements.

As you have seen, there is no easy fix. You must learn and understand the dynamics at all levels and remember to focus your *anger* (energy and focus) on yourself, not others. When you do this, you can harness that energy to improve your situation and improve your relationship with others. You will no longer be hampered by anger. Instead, you will become powerful, driven, determined, influential, and motivated.

To learn more about self-control, mental healthiness, and empowerment, visit Dr. Parker's website www.theparkergroupinc.com or check out his podcast *Just These Guys, You Know?* Dr. Parker teams up with Pastor Mike each week to break down complex matters of life and the spirit in plain language. The podcast is available on YouTube, Apple, Spotify, Podbean, or wherever you get your podcasts. You can read more about *Just These Guys, You Know?* at www.justtheseguys.podbean.com.

And be sure to check out Dr. Parker's other book, *Twelve Two: How to Transform Your Mind*, for a more in-depth look at how to change your thinking and change your life.

Anger-Management Model Template

1. Identify the problem. What is your Primary Emotion, and how would you rather feel in this situation?
   _____
   _____

2. Analyze your perceptions. What are the facts? Any Should statements? Jumping to Conclusions?
   _____
   _____

3. Administer self-care. What can you do to decrease the negative Primary Emotion and increase the preferred emotion?
   _____
   _____

4. Consider if it must be fair. "Really? Everything must be fair?"
   _____
   _____

5. Talk to friends. What advice or feedback do friends give you?
   _____
   _____

6. Talk to clergy. What spiritual advice did your pastor give you?
   _____
   _____

7. Talk with a professional. Any professional input to consider?
_____
_____

8. Communicate Assertively with the person you are in conflict with and truly Listen to them. Take the time to write out what you will say to them. Then imagine how they might respond and plan how you will remain assertive and additional responses that may be effective or necessary.
_____
_____

About the Author

Dr. Parker is a licensed psychologist in Wichita, Kansas. He enjoys riding motorcycles and spending time with his wonderful wife and the greatest son ever. Dr. Parker served in the United States Navy for eight years, began his study of psychology in 1989, earned a bachelor's in 1991, a master's in 1995, a doctorate in 1998, and was licensed in 1999.

Dr. Parker served as the chief psychologist for a nationwide HMO for many years then, in 2005, entered private practice full-time. His work has taken him inside psychiatric prisons, hospitals, jails, and drug rehab centers. Up until 2019, the bulk of his practice centered around forensic psychology, particularly the highly emotional and contentious field of divorce and child custody. Additionally, he has taught anger-management programs since 1999. Dr. Parker is routinely sought out to speak at conferences regarding his expertise in forensic psychology. For years, in addition to his clinical work, Dr. Parker has conducted free seminars and classes designed to demystify psychology and make it useful to people in their everyday life, especially their spiritual lives.

Dr. Parker is most well-known for helping people see how to use simple psychological-reframing techniques to gain control over their mood and to begin developing a true relationship with God.

You can hear more from Dr. Parker on his weekly podcast *Just These Guys, You Know?* available wherever you get your podcasts and YouTube. For more information or to contact Dr. Parker about speaking engagements, visit his website TheParkerGroupInc.com.

Printed in the USA
CPSIA information can be obtained
at www.ICGtesting.com
CBHW031817221124
17856CB00011B/215

9 798894 285627